Out of the
Black Shadows

STEPHEN LUNGU
with
ANNE COOMES

MONARCH
BOOKS

Mill Hill, London & Grand Rapids, Michigan

First published by Monarch Books in the UK 2001,
Concorde House, Grenville Place,
Mill Hill, London, NW7 3SA.

Published in conjunction with African Enterprise.

Distributed by:
UK: STL, PO Box 300, Kingstown Broadway, Carlisle,
Cumbria CA3 0QS;
USA: Kregel Publications, PO Box 2607
Grand Rapids, Michigan 49501.

ISBN 1 85424 554 6 (UK)
ISBN 0 8254 6025 5 (USA)

British Library Cataloguing Data
A catalogue record for this book is available
from the British Library.

Book design and production for the publishers by
Bookprint Creative Services
P.O. Box 827, BN21 3YJ, England
Printed in Great Britain.

OUT OF THE BLACK SHADOWS

CONTENTS

FOREWORD

Stephen Lungu has given a remarkable account of the wonderful dealings of God with him in those years straddling the coming of Independence to Southern Africa. I have been deeply moved to read such a graphic and expressive life story because so much of my life was entwined with his and, later, Rachel's. Never before have I been able to get such a complete picture, and I was especially struck by the intensity of the struggles in the most formative years of his life – some even unwittingly caused by me!

What a testimony to God's grace and power! To me, this is a wonderful demonstration of God's grace in forming a man who never had experienced much parental love or stable family life to become, with Rachel, a wonderful married couple frequently involved in marriage guidance. What an encouragement to any who fear to launch out into serving the Lord because their own lives were so disadvantaged.

Stephen has been most kind in his evaluation of Jill's and my input into his life. We were all much of the same age, and I had so much to learn myself. I bow in adoration before the Lord for all that Africa, and especially my African team-mates, taught me of love, tact, understanding of local culture and walking with the Lord. There were the hard times, the clashes, the growing pains, but these were the foundation of so much of my subsequent ministry. In many ways Stephen was the closest to me of all my African colleagues and my best teacher. I share this here because I do not think Steve has done adequate justice to the fact that the learning was a two-way process!

May this testimony be an inspiration to many and bring much glory to the Lord Jesus!

Patrick Johnstone
WEC International
Author of *Operation World*

PREFACE

Salisbury, Rhodesia, in the spring of 1962, was not the most peaceful of places. The whites had the army, the police and plenty of guns to maintain the right-wing government and the status quo. But they did not have *all* the fighters, or *all* the guns.

The city was riddled with left-wing factions, financed by the Eastern Bloc countries. They wanted control of Rhodesia, and so mobilised a second, secret army and armed it with petrol bombs, hand grenades, Russian rifles and pistols.

Why didn't the government keep this second army out of Rhodesia? Because it was all around them – and potentially made up the majority of Rhodesia. The left-wing groups recruited from the tens of thousands of poor black youths who had little education, few jobs and scanty prospects in life. Most were not politically minded. Like everyone else, these young men simply wanted a better life, food and shelter for their families.

The left-wing groups promised these young men unlimited prosperity. They told them that one day they would have their pick of the white men's belongings, the luxurious bungalows, the glamorous cars. All they had to do was join the 'liberation struggle'. Their enemies were all whites, but especially Christians, for 'obviously' the missionaries had used the Bible to subdue them in the first place.

If you were homeless, jobless, hungry, dressed in rags – and desperate – wouldn't you be tempted?

I was. When the local political agitators found me I was a teenager living on my own under a bridge. My bed was a sandy grave I dug at night, my blanket an old burlap sack. I could not read or write. I could not find a job. The whites had helped me, true – by leaving their rubbish bins unguarded. For years I raided these in order to survive. I wore their cast-off shirts and trousers, and tied their worn-out slippers to my feet with twine. My food came from their rubbish bins as well – slimy porridge, rotting fruit, left-over meat, stale bread.

By day I 'hung out' with other poor black youths. We called ourselves the 'Black Shadows'. We drank beer, did drugs and stole things. The local political agitators urged us, and hundreds like us, to *cause more trouble!*

By the late 1950s and early 1960s the Black Shadows were hard at work in a township of Salisbury. Our instructions were to cause the maximum amount of public terror and civil unrest that we could. We did well, if I say so myself. We threw petrol bombs into white restaurants and peaceful public gatherings. We started riots, urged rebellion, burned police cars. We used our knives to hold people up in the streets and take their money.

I enjoyed it. I had grown up frightened and angry, and at last I felt I was getting my own back. So when one Sunday evening early in 1962 my gang decided to go and bomb a bank in a nearby shopping centre, I looked forward to it. I was delighted to lead the attack.

Shortly after we set out, with our little bags full of

homemade explosive devices, petrol bombs and knives, we came across a huge Christian evangelistic tent meeting. I could hardly believe my luck. To petrol bomb a tent full of several thousand Christians was much better than blowing up a mere bank. I would win a lot of praise!

Hastily I planned the attack, and posted my 'soldiers' at the opening of the vast marquee. Once they'd thrown their flaming petrol bottles, they'd be able to attack the Christians as they came out. I told them I'd give the signal in five minutes. In the meantime, I decided to see what the Christians were doing in there. Carefully holding my bag of explosives, I slipped into the tent.

Because of my curiosity that night, this book came to be written.

CHAPTER ONE

MY UNHAPPY HOME

I lay on the big untidy bed and watched my mother drink beer from her jug. She held it high in both hands, tilting her dark head back, drinking deeply, savouring each swallow. At last she sighed with contentment and lowered the jug to the floor, wiping her lips and chin with the back of her arm.

'Ah,' she breathed. Expertly her calloused toes eased the jug back into its hiding-place under the bed.

A spasm hit me and I coughed, spitting onto the flowered bed-cover. I stuck a grubby fist to my mouth to try and stifle the sound. Mama got cross with me because I coughed so much. She complained to my aunts that I was always sickly. But the pains in my chest had been bad today. When I opened my eyes, her dark eyes were full of exasperated affection – she always felt better after beer.

'Ah Stephen, what can I do with you? You are always, always poorly.' I liked it when she'd had beer, because it made her less cross with me.

'Mama.'

She contentedly stretched out on the counterpane beside me and I snuggled up to her – her warm teenage body and bosom spelled love and contentment for me. She was tiny and very dark and I thought her beautiful.

Outside in the late afternoon heat the hens clucked drowsily to themselves, and some children squealed in play and raised clouds of dust. Some men called to one another. This was 1946 and the black township of old Highfield on the outskirts of Salisbury, Rhodesia, was a quiet place, if very poor.

Mama stroked my hot forehead. 'So where's your father then, eh?' she whispered fretfully, watching the flies on the ceiling. We hadn't seen him for the last few days, and Mama had not been happy about that. 'I have no money to take you to the hospital.'

Papa worked for the government. He was a telephone repair man, based in a post office in Salisbury. Somehow, when he did not come home after work, it made Mama cross with me and John, my two-year-old brother. The following morning she'd stomp off to work in the field with the other women, muttering to herself. She would slap John and me for any little thing as we played near where the women worked.

It was a curious thing, because when my father finally did return, as he always did, Mama never seemed glad to see him. Standing in the doorway, her arms folded across the bosom of her colourful dress, her face would go blacker than ever with anger.

Her marriage to my father, I would learn later, had always been difficult. Mama had been only thirteen years old when he had arrived in Highfield, a man nearly fifty years old, with two marriages behind him. According to traditional custom at the time, marriages were arranged, and for some reason, Mama's parents had decided to give her in marriage to him, much to Mama's distress. Mama had spent the first year of her marriage, even when she became pregnant, running away from her husband, seeking refuge back with her parents. They returned their young daughter every time, forcing her to go back to the husband she did not want. I was born out of this unhappy union, when Mama was only fourteen years old.

'I love you, Mama. Can't we just be happy together?' That was what my four-year-old mind felt, but I was not old enough yet to express it in words.

So I loved these times when she had had some beer, either alone, or with some of her girlfriends. Beer helped Mama forget her misery for a while. It gave her the only comfort she had. The times when she drank beer with me were quiet, contented, dreamy times. She sat quiet and I could get close to her. My brother John, almost two, would play nearby. She'd even cuddle me.

The sun sets swiftly in Africa and our black township of old Highfield experienced a brief flurry of activity as people went to and fro, locking away chickens, looking for children, looking for husbands (often in vain). Women busied themselves with their outdoor cooking fires and men gathered for an evening of beer-drinking as the sun set over the untidy mix of corrugated asbestos roofing and the thatching of the older huts.

Slowly, Mother got up and lit an oil lamp as the smell of cooking fires drifted in. She busied herself outside with the cooking pot, humming softly to herself. In the violet twilight, the bats flitted overhead as they left the forests around the township.

Then we heard footsteps and a neighbour's dog barked, and Mama stiffened and listened intently. I heard them too – a man's footsteps. . . .

Mama rushed into the bedroom and swilled some water in her mouth. My cough was painful. 'Mama!' I held out my arms.

She turned on me with a look that made my words die on my lips. 'You shut your mouth! You're always fussing.'

I began to sob, which made me cough. 'Mama!' I wailed. She came to the bed and grabbed me tight by my upper arms. 'You be quiet! And if you tell him I've been drinking beer, I'll beat you. I'll give you something to really cry about!'

Appalled by her anger, I slid even further under the flowered coverlet, pulling it tight over my head. I watched her through one of the holes in the coverlet.

Mama slid her hands to her hair, and patted it neatly into place. She quickly drank some water, and popped a small onion into her mouth to disguise the smell of the beer. She smoothed her sleeveless cotton frock down over her still slim eighteen-year-old hips. She stared up at the geckos on the ceiling for an instant, composing herself. As she turned to go out of the room, I doubt she even heard my whimpers. The moths, tilting crazily, followed her oil lamp. The geckos watched them go in disappointment.

I lay tense as I heard the footsteps arrive outside our little red-brick house and my father's harsh voice demand, 'Where's my dinner?' as if he had been at work in Salisbury all day and not on one of his periodic disappearances.

My mother's reply was shrill and hostile. I buried my face in the grimy pillow and tried not to hear.

'. . . and Stephen's ill again, and how I gonna call the doctor with no money?'

'That boy is *always* ill,' my father sneered. I closed my eyes and clenched the coverlet tighter as my father stomped into the room. He held the oil lamp high above me. Roughly he pulled off the coverlet and rolled me over onto my back. I opened my eyes and peered fearfully up at him.

My mother was now shrilly defending my right to be ill, though she sounded fairly angry with me as well. 'We could all die and you wouldn't know. You're not even here. You have another woman – I know you do.' She was probably right – Mama knew he'd left his last wife and son behind in Malawi some years before. He'd headed off to the goldmines of South Africa, and simply never gone back to them.

But Father stared down at me as if he were looking for something and could not find it. He wheeled on her. 'Well, why should I be here? Why should I raise this boy? You tell me this is my son. He doesn't look like me at all. I tell you I am not his father.' He had said this before, and it always left me with a very strange lost feeling. 'Who is my papa then?' I would ask myself.

My mother cried protests, but got too close. My father suddenly sniffed suspiciously. 'Eletina, you have had beer,' he snarled.

'No! No! Always you accuse me.'

I lay still, hoping my father wouldn't push his big feet under the bed any further – he'd kick over mama's beer jug. Mother flounced out of the room with him close behind her. My coughs were ignored. As their argument raged in the other room, I lay, wracked with pain, crying silent tears. Silence was safest. My parents got angry when I cried aloud.

* * *

When I awoke next morning, everything was different. The house was quiet. Bright sunlight streamed through the curtains as a cheery breeze rustled them with unseen fingers. Chickens clucked contentedly outside the door.

My father washed and shaved in silence in the basin by

the back door. My mother bustled around the bedroom, smoothing her hair, slipping into her best cotton flowered frock, fussing with a hat. That hat and the tranquility made it a certainty: this must be Sunday. I stretched a little and coughed painfully, but felt content. Today would be all right. On Sundays my parents took a day of rest from fighting, and went to church and smiled at people instead. I had no idea why; I just knew that this was so, and so I liked Sundays.

Mother decided that I was well enough to go to church, and dressed me in my other pair of shorts and shirt – the Sunday ones. She carried John, and Papa swung me high up onto his shoulders. Papa walked in front, as usual. In African tradition, women generally walk behind their husbands.

'Good morning!' he said to all the neighbours we met along the way, flashing his brilliant smile at them with his perfect teeth. Papa was not very tall, but he was slim and fit. In old Highfield no one cared that he was not Rhodesian born and bred – there had been too many new-comers in recent years for that. Thousands of men from Malawi (then called Nyasaland) and Zambia (then called Northern Rhodesia) came to Zimbabwe (then Southern Rhodesia), tempted by the goldmines and burgeoning industry of Rhodesia. Besides, Papa, who was much older than Mama, had a reputation for having seen something of life. Not for nothing was his nickname Chiwaya –'big gun'. He had fought in the First World War.

'Ah, Chiwaya! Eletina!' Neighbours smiled and nodded at my parents. 'Chiwaya, what are you going to preach about this morning?'

My father smiled and looked mysterious. 'Ah, you must wait and see.' He was an elder in our local Presbyterian church, and his thundering, oratorical style made him a popular preacher. Indeed, I once heard one of my aunties say that 'big gun' was a good description of how he preached.

Outside the church a lad was beating a length of rail which had been hung as a makeshift bell. The congregation was very proud of the church with its fresh mud walls and grass-thatched roof. Inside it even had fixed pews, built of bricks.

I lay content in my mother's arms throughout the long sermon as my father berated the congregation in angry staccato bursts. He was good at knowing what people felt guilty about, and got a lot of nods of agreement. I was happy to see him up there in front of everybody. But I was frightened of approaching him at home.

Papa's real name was William Tsoka. Tsoka meant 'unlucky'. This was an apt surname for our family, because in the months that followed, we lost even Sundays as the family truce day.

That happened because the government telecommunications department for whom Papa worked transferred him from Salisbury to a town called Bindura, about eighty kilometres away. Papa had to go. After a loose-jointed career in smallhold farming and then the gold mines of South Africa and Rhodesia, he needed to stick with this job if he was going to get any pension.

Mama was horrified at the news of the move. Although her family was from Zambia, her father had been in the police force in Rhodesia for forty years, and she had been born and grown up in Salisbury. Highfield township was home. Her family were all here. She'd met my papa when he'd arrived from the goldmines of Eiffel Flats in Kadoma, but she'd never had plans to leave old Highfield.

So amid much bitter haggling and rows, we moved to a small bungalow in Bindura. It was miserable from the first day. Mama drank more and more beer to ease her loneliness and misery when Papa was at work. Without the little Presbyterian church at Highfield, Sundays were as full of bitterness and anger as any other day. Mother also began to lose more and more of the arguments. Something was happening to her. She was tired a lot and her tummy was getting bigger and bigger.

But night after night, the rows went on, while John's teething screams soared an octave above the angry voices.

I often seemed to be the focal point of Papa's anger. 'That boy is not my son! We'll see if the next one is!'

Then *who is* my father? I would wonder again and again. Mama would become hysterical in her insistence that I was indeed Papa's son.

'No, he is not. And you, Eletina, are nothing but...' and Papa would pour out a torrent of abuse and hate with as much fervour as he preached.

One night he beat Mama very badly, shoving her against the wall and throwing her across the bed. I tried to stop him. I clung to his leg. He kicked me across the room.

'I'll kill myself!' Mama screamed. 'I will!' She said it like it was the worst thing in the world.

I huddled on the floor, too terrified to move. Kill must be dreadful. What did it mean?

Finally one day, news reached Mama that a relative of hers had died back in Salisbury.

'I'm going home,' she said determinedly. 'For the funeral.' Then she added, as an afterthought, 'And the birth.' What birth?

She packed her bag and put John and me on the bus with her. Papa did not even come to the bus station to say goodbye.

It was a long, hot and weary journey. We stayed with her parents in old Highfield, and there were a few brief weeks of tranquility until Papa returned. The government had changed its mind, and soon we all went back to our little house in Highfield.

Then it was 1947 and I had a new sister. With her arrival, and John now an active toddler, Mama, at nineteen years of age, had little time for me. I spent a lot of time playing in the dust outside our little house. Mama told me to watch my little brother, who at three was already nearly as big as me at five, and eager for mischief. I still coughed a lot, but Mama did not seem to notice any more. Though when I thrust a hot face against her, she would caress me with an absent-minded hand.

Whenever Papa was home, it seemed he was furious with Mama, accusing her of things that I didn't understand, but which made her cry. In return, Mama was furious with Papa, especially when he did not come home at all some nights. I could not understand this, but I began to feel very guilty about it all. It was obviously all my fault that my parents fought. If Papa had thought I was his son, things would have been OK. So it was my fault that Papa did not love Mama. I felt embarrassed by my existence.

Then, when I was about seven, there came a time when Papa was gone for days on end. Mama cried all the time. Lots of aunts visited our house in a flurry of heaving bosoms and indignant cries. I gathered by the end of it all that Papa had been transferred away again by the government, and this time had left us all behind. I kicked pebbles around in the dust. Had it been my fault? I suspected it was. I would try and make it up to Mama. I felt guilty for being alive. I guessed I wasn't his son. Then who was I? I was Mama's son. I went and stood close to her as she wailed with the aunts.

CHAPTER TWO

ABANDONED

One afternoon, some time later, after my aunts left, my mother came out of the house holding my baby sister Malesi in her arms. Mother called to John and me, who were playing in the dust. 'Come along – we are going into town.'

We came along happily. Mother had not taken us out for weeks – mostly she had been cross or crying. That afternoon she seemed distracted, but we trotted along after her, and climbed aboard the bus and off again. We liked the excitement of a walk along the shops on the edge of old Highfield.

It was exciting, but I clung very close to Mama. I held her hand tight, but she didn't look down to speak to me. I tried to get her to look at the sights that caught my eye, but she didn't respond.

Mother didn't seem quite sure where she was going. After walking many busy streets, she took us to the market and paused.

'Mama, look!' I was fascinated by men unloading a lorry of vegetables.

She didn't seem to hear me. 'Come on,' she said, and set

off again, this time past the garage.

That took us to the town square, near a district called Machipisa Shopping Centre. John and I stared round in amazement. Everything looked so vast, so busy. Mama paused and looked around too, as if looking for something or other.

Then she looked down at me and said with an unusual intensity in her voice, 'Stephen, I want you to stay here. Stay here.'

'Mama!' I was aghast. John and I clung to her. But firmly she detached our little fingers.

'No – no – you stay. I must go to – the toilet.' Suddenly she was brisk. 'Stay now!' Then – 'Here,' she added, thrusting my little sister into my arms. I nearly dropped the wriggling bundle of arms and legs. 'Take care of her. And watch your brother – don't let him run off.' She was suddenly upset and cross.

I was used to her changes of mood and trying to appease her. 'Yes, Mama,' I said, staggering slightly under the weight of the baby. My seven-year-old arms tightened round her and she began to cry.

Mother's hand rested briefly on my head, and then she was gone, melting into the crowd in the warm afternoon sunshine. I shifted the baby about, chirped to her to soothe her, and told my little five-year-old brother to stand still.

We waited, watching the people strolling by. But now so many strangers seemed frightening. The baby was heavy. I shifted from one bare foot to the other and looked around for mother.

A little while and still she had not come. My brother stamped round and round in the dust, playing some private game. Then he stubbed his toe, sat down hard, and began to cry. My shoulders were aching by now, and I felt like crying myself. I looked round and round about me. No mother.

I still recall with a shudder those first waves of real fear that swept over me. In a sudden panic, I WANTED MY MOTHER. Where was she? My self-control gave way and I cried. John cried, and Malesi cried.

A long time passed. The afternoon was waning. The sun was slipping towards the brief equatorial dusk. In our fear and anxiety, my brother and sister and I howled in the late afternoon sunshine. We wandered about the square, roaring our misery.

Concerned, adult faces peered down at us, 'Where is your mother, boy?'

'Mama! Mama!' I wailed. John and Malesi screamed along. More adults came over.

'I've watched them – they've been here on their own for a couple of hours,' someone said.

A little while and then a policeman arrived. We were too hysterical to be coherent. So he finally gave up and simply walked us down to the police station. I struggled and peered behind me as we left the square, hoping against hope to catch a glimpse of Mother running towards us. But already the adults had forgotten us, and were moving on about their business. Tranquility had closed over the serene square. A few children had lost their mother. Not worth more than a moment's thought.

'Come along now, boy.' The policeman yanked me along. At last I turned away from the square and stumbled after him. In that moment, at seven years of age, I learned the meaning of utter despair. My mother had broken faith with me. She had abandoned me to – what? She was never coming back. She had rejected us – for no reason that I could understand. I had never told Papa about her beer. How could she do this to me?

Something besides love and fear and hurt entered me at that moment – a monster with which I would have to battle many times in the years to come to stop it consuming me: self-hate and bitterness. My brother and sister were too young for anything, but it bit deep, deep into me. My father had fought with Mama because of me. He must have abandoned us because of me. Now Mama had abandoned me. It must be me. I must be evil for them to treat me so. They must have really hated me. I didn't know what I had done, but I began to hate me too.

The policeman at the desk looked us over with no great happiness. He gingerly picked up Malesi in his arms – sniffed, and quickly set her down again, looking now at the front of his shirt and his hand in consternation. He sighed and said something to another policeman, who took Malesi away. Malesi screamed, and the policeman looked pretty unhappy too. John and I sat on a bench, too terrified and hoarse by now to cry. Soon another man in uniform came to ask us questions. He asked John, and John snivelled and stuck a grubby fist into his mouth. He asked me, 'What are your names? Where is your mother?'

Great tears rolled down my face. 'She left us.'

Later a lady came. She looked at Malesi and shook her head. I heard words like 'too young' and 'poorly' and 'hospital'. She looked at John and me with the same considering look, but this time nodded her head. 'How would you like to go with me to the orphanage home?'

We would *not* like that one bit, but no one took any notice of our fresh floods of tears. We went with the lady to the orphanage home.

There was a long room with beds all along it. John and I were given two together. We cried until we could cry no more.

The people at the orphanage were more skilful at talking to children than the police. Next day they discovered we came from Highfield township and what's more, possessed several aunts. We only knew their first names, but the orphanage folk seemed satisfied, and smiled at us, and urged us to play in the sunshine. John and I sat with our hands across our faces, and peeped timidly through our fingers at the other children.

A day or so later Aunt M arrived at the orphanage, looking unfamiliar in a hat. 'Aunty!' we cried, flinging ourselves on her. She looked less than enraptured to see us.

'You boys. Where's your mother? What's she done then? What am I supposed to do?'

She left us in the hallway and went in to talk to the orphanage people. It went on for a long time. John and I waited anxiously. What was wrong? Aunt M's voice was raised in protest several times.

When black people get angry, they go even blacker. Aunt M was glowering like midnight when she at last came out. She glared at us. 'Good God in heaven, as if I haven't got enough problems.' With plump, strong hands that pinched, she swept us before her and down the orphanage steps into the sunshine.

'Where's Mama? Where are we going?' we said. But Aunt M was so busy talking crossly to herself that she didn't get round to answering.

Aunt M's brick bungalow was only a short walk from our old house, but going there was awful and very different. I felt the whole world had changed. We spent that first afternoon wandering aimlessly about outside with the chickens, or squatting meekly at the doorway of the little house, trying to hear and understand the furious meeting that was underway inside. A veritable congress of aunts – all Mama's sisters – had been called, and all afternoon large distressed aunts swept in and out, bosoms heaving, eyes flashing with indignation that my mother should just dump her children on them.

We were too young to understand then why our aunts were so angry at having to take charge of us. We did not know then that our mama and her sisters had never got on well together, and had always fought. Mama had been the odd one out in her family, the one who got picked on. Now our aunts took their dislike for Mama out on Mama's abandoned children.

No one pretended that they wanted us, so I did not pretend to want them. As the afternoon wore on, I slipped away, and ran like a wild dog through the dusty roads and houses and lorries and cows – back home. It looked the same as ever – the dusty yard, the curtains. I approached it slowly, willing my Mama to suddenly open the door and for everything to be OK again.

The place was empty. I wandered from room to room. Finally I leaned up against the wall, feeling weak and sick. I wanted to die. It was a long time before I stumbled slowly back to my aunt's house.

Back at the aunts' congress, it became clear that a temporary solution was emerging – they would share out the work of caring for us. It was more a case of, 'Well, I can have them this week, but no more!' and the others appealingly muttering, 'OK, OK, just take them for a few days.'

So for several weeks John and I – and soon Malesi – were shunted from aunt to aunt. We slept on dirt floors under bits of old blankets. We ate scraps of all descriptions, both off the table and as we wandered about outside. Then the number of aunts willing to have us at all began to dwindle. Excuses and indignant denials and refusals were heard. More and more we were dumped on Aunt M, who also made no secret of her frustration and anger at having three more children to feed and care for.

My mother was heaven knows where, so Aunt M took out her fury on us instead. She was very strict, and any small lapse on our part was an excuse for her to vent her frustration by beating us. I was beaten very often as soon as her son discovered he could now get away with not watering the garden or sweeping the house, and simply blame it on me. He knew my denials would not be believed.

When the little township school started again that January, she sent me along, mainly to get me out of the way for a while. I was put in the first class, but struggled. I was so unhappy that first day that I even wet my pants. School held little interest for me. Often I played truant, and that put me even further behind. While the other children played hilarious games in the dust, I would tend to wander off round the township, watching the other children and their parents. My mind was full of deep, deep sadness, far sadder than any eight-year-old should ever know: 'Why was I born in that family?' I asked myself many times. I felt there was nothing in the world for me. I felt so insecure, so lost. I wanted to die.

One day my reveries were broken into by a more immediate and pressing problem. I had gone for a walk, and was concentrating on kicking a certain stone along ahead of me when suddenly a group of little boys rushed out from behind a chicken coop and surrounded me.

'You have no mother!'

'You have no father!'

'You're so small!'

As that more or less summed up the situation, no more was said, and the boys waded in with their fists. Fortunately my screams were heard by my brother John, who came plummeting down the lane. At six, he was already much bigger and stronger and more aggressive than me, and thoroughly enjoyed a fight. He rushed in to my defence, shouting blue murder, kicking and fighting.

My tormentors fled, and I picked myself up out of the dust.

'You tell them I'll beat them up if they ever touch you again.' My little brother swaggered off.

They did touch me again, and I did run to my brother, and he was always true to his promise, and went and beat them up. To have one champion in the world – if only a six-year-old brother – was a marvellous boost to the morale. I felt so proud – as if I'd done it myself.

The months went by and one school year ended and turned into Class Two. Having not passed Class One, or learned to read or write words, I now found it very diffi-cult to construct sentences. My problem was temporarily solved in a most unexpected way.

John and I came into Aunty's house one day and stood stock still in utter amazement. Papa was there!

'Papa!' John hurled himself into his arms. He and Papa had always been fond of each other. Papa gave him a great bear hug and nodded to me over John's head. I longed to go close, but felt uncertain what to do. Papa did not reach out for me.

Aunty rocked contentedly in her chair, happier than I had seen her for months. 'Your father's come back. Now you can live with him at your old home.' Malesi sat com-posedly on Aunty's lap, not recognising her own father. It did not matter – Aunty had more or less adopted Malesi.

But Aunt M was wrong about Papa's intentions. Soon he said casually that he had to go and buy a few things in Highfield and that he might as well take us boys along. He took us to the shop but did not stop there. Instead he put us on a bus, and took us to the train station. He put us on the train with him, and without more ado, with only the T-shirts and shorts we stood up in, we were taken to Malawi. It seemed Papa had been pensioned off by the

Rhodesian government, and so had gone home to his native country and had married for the fourth time. I never understood why he came back for us.

Papa's latest wife and his several new step-children eyed us sullenly as we arrived in Salima, a town in central Malawi, near Lake Malawi. They obviously didn't understand why Papa had brought us with him either, and they did not like it one bit. It was not a happy home. Papa treated his new wife harshly, and often shouted at her. She in turn beat me whenever she had the chance in Papa's absence. She left John alone, as he had fought back, and I guess she was a little scared of him.

Papa knew that his new family did not like his two sons, because it meant there was less money to go around. So soon he moved John and me out of the house, and in with his sister instead. His sister, however, resented the fact that his pension was going on yet another wife, and none of it was being shared with her as she had expected it would be. So his sister got her revenge by being cruel to John and me, and we dreaded her coming near us.

'I want to go home,' I confided to some of the village ladies of Salima one day. Compared to beatings in a strange house in a foreign land, Highfield township seemed a blissful sanctuary. I did not stop to think about how my Aunt M might take it.

The village ladies sympathised with how hard it was for me. 'Poor Stephen. Your papa doesn't really want you. Your stepmother *really* doesn't want you. Neither does your aunt. Why don't you go back to Highfield?'

'I have no money for the train.'

'You can sell your bicycle. That would get you a ticket home.'

To them and to my ten-year-old reasoning, this seemed as good a plan as any. They warned me to be especially careful at the border, and then told me how to get to the railway station. A few days later I was off. This time I was abandoning Papa and John. I had no regrets. Papa and John were by now forming a bond of love, but no such bridge had ever been built between my father and me. Their closeness was making me feel a total outsider in my own family. Papa's love for John was destroying my relationship with John. I knew Papa did not love me, and so would not care if I left. And I so badly wanted to go back to Highfield.

CHAPTER THREE

THE CHICKEN COOP

No one took any notice as I crept into the railway station. There were plenty of trains, too. The only tricky part was making sure which one went home to Rhodesia. I hung about near the platform, and the station-master. On the journey up, I'd heard these men shout about the trains. Finally I heard the magic words: Blantyre. I had been told that this was my first connection.

My heart was pounding like a hammer as I approached the train. I had decided to try to get home without a ticket, as the money from the bicycle was all I had in the world. Several doors were ajar, and I crept into the one which lay in the deepest shadows. I was small and very dark and once inside, any adult would have had a job to find me. The goods were piled high in crates all about me.

The only hitch to this sort of help-yourself travel soon arose – there was no food or water. The next day, as the train wound through the countryside stopping at stations under the hot African sunshine, thirst soon drove me out of hiding. I found water at the stations, and desperate begging secured me enough scraps of food to keep me going.

Then I discovered that I could travel with the other passengers. Some motherly women invited me into the carriage with them and their families, and fed me. Whenever the ticket collector came around, I'd simply crawl beneath the benches and hide behind their long skirts.

At last, after several changes of train from Salima to Blantyre, and on through Mozambique, we reached Salisbury. The train pulled heavily, noisily, hot and overladen into the station, like one of my aunties coming in from work in the fields. It stopped amid creaks and groans. Immediately doors flew open and a great commotion began. No one noticed a small boy slip out of one of the wagons, duck between two steaming carriages, and disappear into the chaos of the station.

It was great to be back! I paused in the station and admired the tall white folk go by, followed by porters laden with their luggage. I compared my nondescript dirty shirt and shorts and bare legs and feet to the pristine frocks and white skin of the ladies and white suits of the men. I gazed at them in awe and fascination. Whites were wonderful people – like gods. However did they stay so clean? They didn't seem human at all.

After my international travels, getting back to Highfield (and dodging the fare) was mere child's play, well within my ten-year-old experience. I had tears in my eyes as I wriggled off the bus and away from the ticket man. I'd been so frightened that maybe Highfield would not be here any more. But the township lay serene, shabby and dusty as ever in the late afternoon sun. Chickens, stray dogs and people wandered about. Home. I burst into tears.

Quickly I trotted along to Aunt M's house, keeping a watchful eye out. I had just remembered that John was no longer there to call on if I met the gang of little boys.

Aunty's house looked just the same. There were voices inside. The brief African sunset was nearly over. I paused outside on the path to watch the smoke arise from Aunty's cooking fire. The doorway darkened for an instant as Aunty appeared, cooking pot in hand. She came out, tended to the fire, and then realised the little boy at the end of her path was not moving on. She looked up, irritated, about to chase me off, and then recognised me.

'Aunt M?' My lips formed the words, but only a whisper came as I caught the look of horror and disbelief on her face.

She clumsily got to her feet. 'God in heaven!' she screamed. 'Not you! No!' She strode down the path and caught me as I shrank away from her. Her eyes consumed me as if she simply could not believe what she saw. 'Stephen!' she spat. 'What are you doing here?'

'I didn't like it with Papa. So I came – home,' I ventured.

'Home!' She shook me, and clipped me on the side of the head. I cried and struggled. Suddenly a dam of fury burst inside her. With incredible strength she held my arm with one hand and pummelled me and scratched at my face with fingers like claws. Finally breathless, she threw me to the ground. 'How dare you come back to me!' she panted. 'After your papa . . . .' Words failed her, and so she kicked me.

Then she spotted the chicken coop. She bent and grabbed an ear and hauled me, screaming, to my feet.

'You are not coming into my house no more! I will not have it!' She strode over to the coop, pulling me along behind her. Quickly she undid the latch, stepped aside, and thrust me in. I fell to the ground, sobbing, and she locked the door.

'You wretched boy! You stay there! Don't think you have a place in my house!'

The chickens, alarmed, clucked and fluttered as I sobbed myself out. Finally I gingerly moved around the coop. I came across the remains of a burlap sack among the chicken feathers and droppings, and gratefully wrapped it around my shoulders. My teeth were chattering with shock and the cool onset of night. The train had been warm and cosy, if stuffy. Later that evening Aunty relented enough to feed me by the simple process of tipping some supper scraps over the wire fencing.

Next day Aunty had calmed down somewhat, and let me out with the chickens. In the days that followed we fell into a new, uncomfortable routine. Aunty did not want me, but since I'd come back, and she could not return me to Malawi, she could not altogether bring herself to throw her nephew onto the streets. So a sort of uneasy compromise developed. In return for household chores like sweeping, fetching water and cleaning the chicken coop, she let me stay at nights – sometimes under a bit of blanket on the floor in a corner of the house, sometimes, if she was in a bad mood, back in the chicken coop. But during the daytime when my jobs were done, she did not want me around, and told me to clear off. No more was ever said about school.

I was glad to leave the house during the day, as the scraps of food she threw my way were not enough, and I was desperate to find food.

One day, several months after my eleventh birthday, I set off as usual. Food that morning had been more meagre than ever, and I was ravenous. But all that morning I scavenged about the township in vain. I was squatting, dispirited, by a group of men drinking, when another man came up. He had on a pair of worn leather shoes, and everyone admired them.

'My boss, he threw them away. I fetched them out of his dustbin – he'll never know.' The man turned his feet to and fro with pride. 'You would not believe what them whites throw away! Shoes, clothes, food . . . .

Food!

I rocked dizzily on my heels. The man carried on talking, but the conversation turned to other things. I dared not ask for details, but I was bursting with excitement. Was it possible that the white people threw food away? Surely not. But that man had said so, and he worked as a servant to one of the white families. I had never actually been to a European quarter of Salisbury, but along with everyone else, I knew where they were.

I hovered for a bit, hesitant and frightened at the idea of leaving my township. Hunger drove me at last to walk the long distance to one of the white neighbourhoods on the outskirts of the city.

Nobody wasted a glance on me as I slipped up the wide avenue. In deep, lush gardens, I saw bungalows that looked to me like palaces, and which quite took my breath away. (I also discovered many whites kept large barking dogs.) It took a bit of scouting around, but finally I discovered that there were sort of service slip roads which ran along the back of the houses next to which the servants left the rubbish bins for collection.

My first 'white' rubbish bin! I approached it wide-eyed, still convinced that a guard would rush out at me if I touched it, and arrest me. But nobody was around. Gingerly I lifted off the heavy lid, half expecting a gorgeous meal waiting for me. Instead, a ripe, rotting smell swept up at me, and I retched. An ooze of garbage and household rubbish lay before me. But there must be food down there somewhere, I thought. I found a stick and poked around. There were some oranges green with mould, some indeterminate slimy stuff, and then – there – a dollop of porridge from someone's breakfast. Still nauseous from the stench, I stuck a finger into the gooey mess.

It was clammy. It tasted like porridge mixed with rotting vegetables. I wolfed it down, and prodded away with my stick until I found some more. But the stench of rotting and decay was overwhelming, and I was very sick in some bushes. I lay on the ground and heaved and sobbed. Mama. Mama. If you had not left me. . . .

But no mother came to kiss away my tears, and after a while I decided to try another dustbin. Happily, there were several slices of burnt toast in this one, wedged in some tea leaves and a half-eaten mango. This time I decided to eat away from the smell. I broke the burnt toast into little pieces, wiping away as many of the tea leaves as I could – they got on my tongue and were bitter. The toast was terribly dry, and I was thirsty, so I had a nibble at the bit of mango, and that was a great success. I cheered up, especially when two dustbins down, I found a bone with shreds of meat still on it.

By then the afternoon was well advanced, and I did not want to be caught in a European suburb when it got dark, so I made my way home. For the first time since I could remember, I did not feel hungry.

Aunty was cross again that night, and so I ended up in the chicken coop under my sack, but even so I slept and felt warmer somehow.

In the months that followed I spent a lot of time in the European dustbins. It never occurred to Aunty to send me back to school. Throughout my eleventh year, I got to know the European suburbs nearest Highfield very well indeed, and especially which dustbins provided the most reliable take-aways. I always kept myself out of sight as much as possible, and was careful to put the lids back on, and no one ever seemed to bother about me. One day I picked up a dustbin lid that hadn't been on securely, and discovered an enormous rat. I didn't fight him for the sticky mess that he fancied. Another time, a servant found me being sick on some rotten meat I'd sampled, and moved me on.

I got used to some pretty disgusting sights, but I could never get used to the smell – it made me retch every time. After I'd eaten whatever I could – I simply could not stand the taste of the really rotting meat and vegetables – I loved to wander down the wide avenues of trees and admire the vast bungalows sprawling in their verdant gardens. I looked in awe at the black servants, attired in immaculate white, coming and going soundlessly. What it must be to work in such a place and to wear such a white coat! I dreamed that one day I might do such a thing, but knew I'd never make it. Such an elegant life wasn't for guys like me.

One ambition that seemed slightly less impossible was work as a caddy at the wonderful golf club nearby. I had discovered it early on in my explorations and spent many an hour with my nose pressed against the fence, watching the older black boys in their mid-teens, proudly waiting for their particular white gentleman to come out of the clubhouse and begin their game of golf.

At first these lads loftily ignored me, but as the weeks and months went by, and I crept closer, they would let me join their group so that I could admire them and be suitably impressed by what they said.

One day a white gentleman came out, and for some reason I caught his eye. He looked me over, and asked me to caddy for him. I could scarcely believe it, and drew myself up to the full of my very insignificant height.

'Oh yes, sir!' I said proudly, wishing my shirt did not have quite such a large rip in it.

He motioned to his bag of clubs, and set off. I bent to lift them and follow, and hit a snag. They didn't lift. I heaved and struggled until my eyes nearly popped. I managed to shuffle them along a few paces before dropping them on my foot. I hopped about in pain, still desperately pushing at the bag – a case of the irresistible force meeting the immovable object. I scarcely dared look up as the white gentleman, realising his clubs were not following him, returned. He would be angry and I didn't want him to see my tears of defeat.

Instead, kindness rained down on me. 'Oh dear, boy, have I packed too many golf clubs for you? Never mind. You are a brave lad for trying, and soon you'll be big enough. And – have some change anyway.' He dropped some silver into my hands that blurred as tears of relief filled my eyes. I looked up in amazement. It was the first time a white person had ever spoken to me. I thought he was wonderful.

When the other lads realised I wasn't going to be a threat to this source of their income, they let me in on a secret. 'Stephen, why not go over to the tennis club and collect the balls? You get money for that too.' The tennis club was nearby.

A tennis ball was a cinch after golf clubs, and by the time I was twelve I was a raging success at my new career. I tried to anticipate where the players were going to mis-place the ball, and learned some basic principles. If it was a man playing, the ball was usually further or slightly off angle from where he'd meant it to go. Some men hit it in a particular direction more often than not, usually sending a lot of blasphemy after it. But with the lady beginners, the ball would seem to take on a life of its own, and might go in literally any direction. Once a ball went straight up and came down on a young lady's head – to the astonishment of us both.

'You OK, miss?' I asked anxiously.

'I think . . . so.' She blinked dizzily.

I loved the tennis and golf club. It became my second home, and for the first time since mother had left, I felt I belonged somewhere.

Eventually I earned myself enough to buy a new shirt. This was both a necessity – and a great mistake. My one and only shirt would not have held on to my shoulders much longer anyway, but even so, when Aunty saw I had a source of income, she was electrified.

That night she had me into the house, and settled herself in her chair, standing me before her. She demanded the full story of what I had been up to. (She had never before bothered to ask where I spent my days.) She didn't get much detail from me, but my few disjointed sentences soon convinced her that I must be earning regular money on the tennis circuit.

'You are a wicked boy, Stephen,' was the conclusion. 'That money belongs to me.'

'No!' I was flabbergasted.

'Yes! I've got to feed you and your sister.' Malesi was not an adorable baby any more, but a fractious little girl who had now joined me in the 'nuisance' category.

I was outraged. 'It's my money! I need it!' Earning a few pennies a day was my sole aim in life. How dare she demand it from me.

'I need it too! Give me what you have earned!'

'No!'

'You wicked boy! Come here!' She swooped on me.

'No!'

That was another chicken coop night, my ears ringing with the hard slaps she'd given me. I was used to the chicken coop and the beatings by now, but this demand on my money awoke something new in me that night: real resentment and anger. Perhaps it was the onset of puberty.

But no longer was I a terrified, bewildered child. I was a resentful, angry adolescent. I felt real hatred that night – the strength of it kept me warm and awake for hours.

CHAPTER FOUR

THE BRIDGE

The following day at the tennis club, I was slow and sullen – and so inattentive that I even got hit by the ball.

'What's the matter with you?' the other lads demanded.

'Nothing,' I shrugged. Then: 'My aunt wants my money.'

'Don't give it to her,' was the prompt verdict. But it wasn't very helpful. For in the days that followed I discovered this was easier said than done. My aunt had missed a great career in the security police. She had a genius for being able to hold you, hit you and frisk you for cash, all at once. I was more and more sullen. The worm was turning.

One day we boys had earned a great deal more than usual – the beginner ladies had been playing, sending balls all over the place. After the game, the ladies had staggered off to the clubhouse to recover, and we stretched out on the cool grass. My friends had great plans for their pennies. Some bought cigarettes, some booze. There were several that even bought drugs. That didn't interest me yet, but I liked half-smoked cigarette butts.

'Poor Stephen – your aunty will have it all,' said one friend patronisingly. His parents never took his money. He lit a cigarette.

Then someone said, 'Why go home? I don't – not always.'

I was thunderstruck. Not go home! 'But where would I go?'

'I sleep under the bridge sometimes,' said one lad. 'I'm going there tonight. Come with me.'

I felt excited. Escape from Aunt M! But by the end of the day my friend had forgotten his offer, and force of habit sent me home. I went very reluctantly. I had made many pennies, and was determined to hold on to them.

It was very late afternoon by the time I reached Aunty's house. I heard her scolding her husband and then a scream as she slapped Malesi. Tonight she was in a bad mood. From experience this meant the chicken coop for me.

For what seemed like an age I hovered about, torn with indecision. I was frightened by even the idea of a night spent out in the open on my own. I was twelve years old. I hovered as the brief twilight came and went, bringing the night and the cooking fires. As long as I was sort of near it wasn't so awful. Of course, the later it got, the more sure my fate in the chicken coop became. I hated it in there. I hated everything. I wanted to die, but didn't know how to stop living.

At last I stumbled away into the night. Of course I'd left it too late by now to find any friends or bridges. I heard noises in the darkness and was so terrified that I climbed up into a mango tree and huddled, panting with fright, against the trunk. The leaves of the tree around me helped to shut out some of the vastness of the sky. I spent a cold and uncomfortable night propped up against the branches. I was glad when the birds began their dawn chorus and the first light lit the sky. I felt so desolate that tears trickled down my cheeks.

I wandered down to the market in the early half-light,

and squatted, shivering, just glad to be among people again. All about me men prepared their vegetables for selling. I ate some over-ripe bananas and as my spirits rose, reconsidered the night. It had two supreme advantages over Aunt M's hospitality – I was not smeared with chicken droppings, and I still had my precious money.

As the morning wore on, I visited the European dustbins on my way to the tennis club – where I spent the money on cigarettes and beer, and slept the afternoon away like a dead thing in the warm sunshine.

I went back to Aunty's that night. She gave me many slaps and little to eat, so I decided to try another night out again soon. This time I planned a bit better, and explored some local bridges for a suitable residence.

When I next earned a few bits of silver, I decided to try again. After a visit to the dustbins and the market leftovers, I found a sack at the market, and at twilight headed for a bridge. I crept beneath it, lay down and rolled up in my sacking. But I hadn't counted on the wind rushing about, catching and clawing at me with bitter fingers. I lay and shivered, snuggling deeper into the sand. Finally I sat up, and dug a sort of hollow grave in the sand, scooping it out with chilled fingers. I lay down again in the hole, pulled the sack over me, and carefully swept the sand back over me. That acted as some sort of shelter, and I dozed fitfully, the huge African stars wheeling slowly above my head. I wondered fearfully how I would ever survive to grow up.

I rarely cried any more, but always I had a constant deep fear in me. I did not want to live, but I did not know how to stop living, and I was frightened that one day I would not survive, and starve to death. With the constant hunger and fear and my cough, I always felt unwell.

I did not expect to live to grow up. I saw the future as

one long lonely struggle on my own. I felt so alone and scared. I did not see how life could ever get any better. I found I could not plan – fear of thinking ahead panicked me. I could not concentrate on things. All my life was focused on mere survival. Even planning a few hours would have panicked me.

The stars were so close – they reminded me of the God at the little Presbyterian church. They had talked about his love for people. I felt angry that he obviously did not care any more for me than my parents did.

The next morning I was gritty with sand. There was nothing for it but to wash – I was more camel coloured than black. I crept down to the river and stripped, quickly scrubbing my shirt and shorts on the gravel bank. I had a short swim, shivering, and stretched the clothes on a bank while I modestly hid in some bushes until they were dry. Then I headed back for the 'white' dustbins and my after-noon visit to the tennis club.

It was the beginning of a very bad couple of years for me. My constant inner fears increased when I realised that not only was Aunty M not upset that I didn't go home every night, she was relieved. In fact, she was soon quite cross whenever I turned up, desperate for food – all the dustbins a glutinous mass of rotting and maggot-ridden food in the rainy season.

By the time I had somehow reached thirteen years of age or so, she considered me quite old enough to find food on my own. But at thirteen I was terrified that there was no one in the world to whom I could turn. Living rough makes some youngsters self-confident and street-wise. Not me. I constantly longed for security, for somewhere I would be able to relax and be safe. I ached to be loved by my family – the people who should have loved me but did not. This bothered me a lot – I had a great sense of loss.

So I struggled along as best I could. When my light tennis shoes finally split – I was growing now – I salvaged a
pair of men's ancient carpet slippers from a 'white' dustbin. They were far too big, but better than nothing, and I
spent an afternoon working out the best way to tie them
onto my feet with bits of twine. The slippers gave my feet
protection, but I shuffled and flapped and the boys at the
tennis club laughed when I tripped trying to chase the
balls. One white lady glanced at my feet incredulously, and
turned away with a frown of distaste.

That scared me even more. Without the money here I
would die. I tried not to shuffle, and in the end, tore the
slippers off and ran about barefoot. But I tied them back
onto my feet as each night fell – and I crept away to find
shelter, frightened of the cold and dark, of the bridges, the
mango trees and occasionally the half-finished houses in
which I slept. I would lie awake for hours. But I was even
more frightened as the sun came up each morning: how
would I survive the day? I wanted to run and be a little
boy and have a mama again – but there was no place to
run to. It was a constant living nightmare.

The lads at the tennis club were my only source of
human companionship. They accepted me as no one else
did, and became my substitute family. Through them I
learned everything I knew – and I fear much of it was not
good. I eagerly shared in the occasional opportunities to
smoke marijuana and cigarettes, even to sniff glue and
drink booze. The few hours of oblivion they brought were
wonderful.

By now I had discovered another form of escape from
the sordid poverty of my life – the local cinema in the Cyril
Jennings Hall in old Highfield. The older boys first took
me along with them. The cinema knew its clientele, and
showed mostly American westerns. For the first time I dis-

covered escapism, and I was transported. For a brief hour or two I could shelter in the warm security of the cinema and be taken to a world of wealth, daring-do and excitement, where the good guy, the underdog, always won. The violence and fighting and winning were exciting! I would have given my soul to be a cowboy in the Wild West, and not to be a destitute black orphan on the streets of Salisbury. I accepted all the films as being the complete, literal truth. Nobody told me anything different. How I longed to exchange my ragged slippers for shining leather boots, my ragged T-shirt and shorts for leather trousers and jacket. I was fascinated by the cowboys' guns, and how they twirled them around their trigger fingers. I wanted to stand tall and scare people when I twirled a gun.

Instead, my friends and I acquired knives, which we honed to razor sharpness. We spent hours practising at throwing them, and stabbed many a tree trunk in mock murder. We fantasised about killing people. The power that violence brought was the only way we were likely to survive to grow up on the streets of Salisbury.

About this time the flow of shillings at the tennis club began to dry up. For several weeks there were fewer games. The rainy season was upon us. The friendship of us boys soon evaporated in the heat of competition for the dwindling share of the market. No one could afford any more drugs or trips to the cinema. Some of the boys began visiting their families in the townships more often, in search of food. A great bitterness and sense of loss obsessed me. I was also terrified. I had been carrying a burden far beyond me for too long. I was so scared. No one in the world cared for me.

One day, when the dustbins crawled with maggots, and the tennis club was silent, I turned to Highfield in desperation. Perhaps my aunt, whom I had not seen for weeks, would feed me, just this once. I made my way there tentatively.

Odd – it was mid afternoon but my aunt was sitting outside on a mat that served as her verandah between the house and the chicken coop. As I came around the corner of the house, I could see she was talking to someone. But I just shuffled across to her, asking for food. I had smoked some marijuana and sniffed some glue that morning, and felt a bit muddled.

Then my gaze fell upon Aunt M's visitor, who sat beside her on the mat. She was very short and very dark. She and I stared at each other. Suddenly, I could not breathe.

'Stephen, greet your mother,' Aunt M said dryly.

Mother. My mother, sitting here, plump and well before me. After years of whimpering, of fear, of missing her, here she was. She had left me to die, for all she cared. I had thought I still wanted her, still loved her. Suddenly I realised that I hated her with all my heart.

A knife lay handy in my pocket. It was an okapi knife – so lethal that they were later banned by the government. I snatched it out, clicked to make the blade spring forth, and hurled it at her. She dodged and rolled off the mat into the dust, screaming. It missed her by inches. She screamed again. 'Stephen!'

I turned and fled, my slippers flap-flapping, pounding up the dust. I found a remote hidey-hole under a bridge and curled up, shivering and sobbing uncontrollably. I wished, how I wished, that I had not been born her son. I lay awake all that night, not only frantically hungry, but aware that from now on I could never go back even to Aunt M, no matter what. She would never forgive me that.

In the morning hunger drove me to the market. I tried to steal some bananas and nearly got beaten up. The shock of seeing my mother turned to a deep depression that settled about me. Though I finally found some slimy scraps in a 'white' dustbin that afternoon, I had lost the will to fight on. A great hopelessness engulfed me. No one cared if I was alive or dead. I was constantly so afraid of everything, and there was absolutely no one in the world to turn to. No money, no help: feed yourself or die.

So one day soon after this, I decided to die.

I wondered if I would meet God. Well, if I turned up on the other side before he was expecting me, that was his fault – he and my mother and everybody had made it clear I wasn't wanted down here.

How to kill myself? Stabbing or cutting would hurt. Dying of hunger took too long. My knowledge of the American Wild West came to the rescue. Hanging was the proper way to do it. So I took a bit of rope I had found on a building site, and walked a little way into the thick bush surrounding the township. I found a large rock by a tree at the edge of the Mukuvisi River, near to the hiding place my friends and I used among the rocks. With some little trouble I managed to climb onto the rock and swing the rope over a branch of the tree, nearly falling off and breaking a leg in the process. I knotted it as best I could and put the loop around my neck.

I paused for a second and thought – no more worry, no more trouble. I closed my eyes. I could still see my mother's face as I threw that knife. The old bitter longing and sense of loss swept over me. I wished again that I had been born to a woman who had wanted me. My mother hated me. My father hated me. I hated me too. I was no good to anybody, and too scared to live any longer. I felt hot tears of despair and futility scald my face.

I jumped.

Had I mastered the art of American cowboy knots, this story would have ended then. But my noose was clumsy, and would not tighten enough. I was only half choked, and soon kicking frantically, while darkness clouded over my eyes and my ears rang.

Then hands grabbed my legs and took the pressure off my neck. I heard women's voices, all scolding, all scared, and then somehow the rope was gone and I was lowered gently to the ground.

Dark, concerned faces of women swam above me. 'What are you doing, boy? Don't you know you could kill yourself that way?' 'Quick – get a doctor!' I was heaved up and half dragged along, a leg here, head there, and couple of arms round about me, much like an awkward bit of the firewood which the women had come out to collect when they had spotted me hanging. Then one of the stronger women simply picked me up, slung me over her shoulder, and carried me off to the main road to get help.

Well, my attempted suicide earned me the most luxurious two weeks I had ever known in my fourteen years of life. I was rushed to the casualty department of the local government hospital. After a peevish policeman tried in vain to find out where I came from (after the knife incident, I didn't want them to get in touch with Aunt M), he told me off, and I was properly admitted to the hospital. The nurses and doctors set to work on me. If I had died and woken up in heaven, the contrast between this and my previous existence could hardly have been more pronounced.

To begin with, there were soft words and attention. Nobody shouted at me. I was given kindness, a pat on the head by one of the black nurses. Then the white doctor arrived and gravely examined me. I was terrified, but he asked me questions in a gentle voice and was kind. Next day he even brought me a little toy. The first and last I ever had. Unfortunately, I was too much in awe even to play with it.

Then there was the bed – and such a bed! High and wide and so white and clean. It had a mattress several acres across, covered in spotless soft sheets – all for me. I had never slept between sheets before. Then there were two great soft white pillows. I had never had a pillow before, and did not know what they were for at first.

Then there was the food! Fresh, not over-ripe. No maggots to watch out for. Smelling good! Warm, on plates. I had not tasted hot food for years. There was also a knife and fork, but I ignored those – what with one thing and another I had never learned how to use them.

Then there was the bath! It came as a great surprise, as I'd never had a bath in anything but a river before. At first I feared they were going to drown me – why, I can't imagine. But the black nurses held me firmly and scrubbed and scolded me in a cheery way and, apart from my embarrassment at being bathed by women, I almost enjoyed it.

Then – unheard of luxury – a pair of hospital pyjamas. I had never had pyjamas before, and thought they were wonderful.

For two weeks this unbelievable paradise continued. I made shy friends with the nurses, and on my part, the emotional attachment in return for their care was real. I longed for love, and they gave me more than I had ever known. As far as I was concerned, I was going to stay here for good. With all a boy's impulsive optimism, I thought I could. After all, I'd been ill, and I was now in hospital. No one had ever told me that people have to leave hospital.

But of course, the blow fell. One evening as the nurse was tidying my bed and bringing my dinner, and I was sitting up in blissful anticipation as to what might be on the menu, she said: 'Well Stephen, we'll miss you after tomorrow.'

'Why?' I gaped at her.

'Doctor says you're quite recovered now and that you don't need to stay any longer.' She plumped my pillows.

I clutched at her arm in sudden panic and tried to assess the situation. So it was not enough to have *been* ill to be in hospital. You had to continue being ill.

'I am not well at all, Sister,' I said desperately. 'I am seriously ill.'

But she shrugged off my fingers and flashed her dark eyes at me in a knowing fashion. 'No. Don't be silly. You are well now.'

I gulped down my delicious dinner in a panic. I decided that there must be no more moving around the bed and joking with the nurses when they went past. Campaign STAY IN HOSPITAL was now on.

So for the rest of the evening I lay in bed and groaned loudly whenever a nurse went by. My unearthly wails startled a few of the younger nurses for a moment, but soon it was: 'Oh, do lie still Stephen and stop waking everybody up. . . . No I won't take your temperature again – it was normal half an hour ago. You are not ill!'

'I am ill! I am! This is very serious,' I kept saying as they went by. But my temperature, pulse and colour remained disappointingly normal. The thousands of other symptoms I suddenly developed in my stomach, head, chest and legs were ignored.

So the next day after breakfast they discharged me. They could not have had a more reluctant or more successful patient recovery.

It was a bright sunny morning. I stood outside the hospital, desolate and hating that old feeling of fear. It was like a cloud that settled on me as soon as I left the building. No more hospital food, it whispered. What will you eat today?

Who knew? Not I.

Despair, like a fog, enveloped me. Not even the doctors

or nurses wanted me. Even their kindness had been false, then. I hated myself, convinced that everybody else did too.

I wanted out, and the only way was to die. But suicide had not worked. The policeman had really been quite cross with me – threatened me with arrest and prison if I tried again.

Suddenly that gave me an idea, also based on the American Wild West films. What, after all, was so bad about getting caught? You would at least get meals. I knew – they always fed them in prison in the movies. And if I did something bad enough, like killing someone, then the police would catch me, feed me and hang me themselves. All I had to do was sit back and sleep and eat until they got round to it.

I wandered into the market, turning my new plan over and over in my mind. I could find no fault in it, not at four-teen, with four months' education behind me. In fact, I began to feel the faint glimmerings of a solution to my problem. I would steal another knife from somewhere. I would find an easy victim – anyone, really, I did not mind. And then I would kill him. I would make sure the police caught me. Then they would care for me until they killed me. Problem solved!

CHAPTER FIVE

THE 'BLACK SHADOWS'

Fortunately for the innocent residents of Salisbury that morning, I had no luck in attacking anyone. Depressed and aimless, I finally headed out again to the golf club. As I stretched on the grass with my friends, I was sullen and distracted. After the brief taste of comfort at the hospital, it was unbearable to be thrust out on my own again. I hated everyone at the hospital. I hated myself. I wanted to die.

'Where you been?'

'Around.' I decided it wasn't cool to have attempted suicide and failed.

'You haven't been under the bridge.'

I was startled. 'How do you know?'

Well, it turned out that family problems – new baby, drunken father – had made two of the boys decide to look elsewhere, and a third had joined them.

'We thought we'd join you.'

I was staggered – and heartened. The four of us under the bridge that night was a great deal more cheerful than being on my own.

I lay awake in my sandy 'grave' under my sack and thought: I still want to die. I still want the police to kill me.

So I will still murder someone. But maybe I'd have some violent fun first. Like they did in the American Wild West films. That spurred me on into vague dreams of a contest with the police, where I would be the hero who would go out at the end in a blaze of glory.

Well, it wasn't exactly John Wayne or the OK Corral, but in the following weeks our motley collection of ragged, homeless, illiterate teenagers did form into a sort of gang. We decided we needed a name. After some thought, we chose the most dangerous, romantic name we could think of: the Black Shadows. One of my friends had got it from a Wild West film. It sounded vaguely threatening, and that was good enough for us.

We were keen to prove ourselves, desperate to belong. Other lads soon wanted to join us as well. This was the only family most of us knew. We bought bigger knives. We modelled ourselves on bits we'd heard about other gangs, plus anything that occurred to us. The main thing was always to act big and tough, and never to show pity. Pity to us was weakness. Love was not compassion, but weakness. Love for us was understood only in terms of loyalty to the Black Shadows.

As the weeks went by, we became so involved in the gang that we were reluctant to go anywhere on our own. Walking alone you felt exposed and vulnerable. Whereas, with the Black Shadows around you, you felt safe, big, important.

But how did people become a Black Shadow? We decided to sharpen up some proper initiation rites for our gang. So we spent an afternoon up at the golf club (where we still meekly caddied for the white folk) and an evening down in the market, standing around, arguing over what these should be.

The aim, everyone agreed, was to prove how brutal we

were. Just then an old lady walked by. Suddenly we decided a perfect example would be to find an old woman (always black – to us, whites were still from another planet) and kick away her walking-stick. One of us lads tried it out on the old lady there and then. When she fell she started screaming. Her screams and fear delighted us. My friend walked on her and kicked her, and we ran off, congratulating each other.

We arrived breathless at the far end of Machipisa Shopping Centre – and immediately the brutal attack on an innocent old woman was chosen as a rite of passage into the gang.

Another rite of passage was that of mixing our blood together. We each cut our arms to get some blood, and then mixed the blood together. This made us blood brothers – all members of the Black Shadows together. I took this rite very seriously.

As I look back now, one thing was for sure: we had changed from being brutalised children to becoming vicious teenagers. Teenagers are above all pack animals – the peer group comes first and foremost. All of us had either been abandoned by our parents, or else our parents were street beggars. We felt outcasts from society and so now, in defiance, we stuck together. The bonds of our gang were strong. Individually, each one of us was weak and defenceless, but together we felt we could defy the harsh world around us. The gang became our only identity. It became my family. My gang friends were rough and rude at times, but still all I had.

Of course, we were eager to use our knives. Our first muggings, in which we threatened our victims to gain their wallets or valuables, were the test of manhood for us all. Now, we felt, we would not only survive, but control the streets.

My first stabbing was a moment of high drama for me. For the first time in my life I felt I had power over somebody else. But all night under the bridge I relived it. I had nightmares. Though I had not badly injured the man, I could not get his frightened face out of my mind, and it haunted me. I felt restless and ill. My tossing to and fro and muttering in my sleep disturbed my friends, who guessed what was wrong.

'The only solution, Steve, is to do it again. Keep on doing it, and you'll get over it!' was the counsel of my friends next morning. And they were right – after another few stabbings, I did find it easier and easier to live with.

In the months that followed, we attacked many other men, usually on Friday nights, which was payday in the city. We wanted their wallets. So we would follow lone men down quiet alleys or lanes and then threaten them with our knives, and feel a thrill when we saw the fear in their eyes. To savour this power was the main delight for us. Provided they did not fight back, we let them go unharmed. Some of my friends attacked and robbed women, and even raped them in front of me. I did not think much of this, and would laugh uneasily while the women screamed for mercy. Their helpless tears upset me, and I wanted my friends to finish and let them go quickly.

But soon I was falling ill again, and in the months that followed I spent many days shivering with fever under the bridge, or lying listlessly in the sun while the Black Shadows went foraging. They were becoming wilder and wilder. They began by robbing car radios. Then they stole the cars themselves, including a Rolls Royce, which got them into trouble with the police. I listened to their stories with great excitement. I was proud to be a Black Shadow. The poor black townships of Salisbury were the only world we knew, and surviving in them our only ambition.

Human life here was cheap, and we were determined we would not be the ones to go under.

By now it was the late 1950s and I was in my mid-teens. I was waking up to the fact of the political tensions in Rhodesia. Men said that our country should not belong to the whites or be called Rhodesia. It was a black country, our country. True patriots should join the struggle for the liberation of Zimbabwe. The Liberation Struggle, it was called. It was a first recruitment, done by local people, for the National Democratic Party, but it was financed by communist interests from outside the country.

The idea of black supremacy in Rhodesia had great appeal to millions of our people, of course, but it was especially attractive to young, poor, homeless lads like us. It gave our anger and general frustration a focal point, an ideal to fight for.

Many of the lads I knew were immediately attracted to the idea of being trained to fight for the liberation of Zimbabwe. I went along to one of the first meetings held at a house in Highfield. We went in one by one, every half hour or so – the government had prudently banned any group meetings of blacks.

The mysterious stranger who was there to recruit us had a stirring message: fighting was the only way to liberate the country from the white oppressor. If we were willing to fight for our country, they would train us how to do so. We would learn how to use the weapons of general civil disruption: petrol bombing, rioting, the sabotage of banks, post offices, beer halls, and government-run institutions, etc. Anything to give the government a major headache and a lot of work.

Everybody thought this was a great idea. I agreed, and said so many times, but somehow did not get round to doing anything about it for months. For one thing, I lacked the self-confidence of many of my friends. Why should anyone want me in the Youth League of the NDP? Also, deep down, I was not a political animal, and my main concern was simple personal survival. Life was a continuing misery of trying to find food, and any beer or marijuana was welcomed for the temporary oblivion it gave me. I hardly felt strong enough to fight to stay alive, never mind take on the powerful white government of the land. I was still too frightened by daily life to have time for political anger.

So while the lads were actively talking about joining the liberation struggle, I hesitated – until two incidents happened which gave me the anger I needed.

The first took place one day when, out of a fit of nostalgia, I paused while going past the little Presbyterian church my parents had taken me to so many years before. It seemed a lifetime ago. As I lingered there in the sun, a man in a dog collar and suit came out.

'What do you want?' he asked suspiciously.

I resented being thought of as a passing stray and said nonchalantly, 'I was brought up at this church. My father used to preach here – before you came.'

The man looked at me with sudden interest. I cheerfully enlarged on my story for his benefit, until I had painted a picture of my family and me as earnest and devout churchgoers – the pillars of the church for many years.

'Would you like a job?' came the surprising request.

Why not? I was flattered by the interest in his eyes, and ready for anything. This might be an adventure.

The job consisted in sorting church membership cards. 'As you know all the people, this will be easy for you,' said the pastor.

'Oh. Yeah. Sure.' I forced a smile, and then frowned at the cards. I could remember just enough of my alphabet to make out some letters and so I puzzled away at them for several mornings. It would be good to earn some money. The only tricky moment came when I was caught smoking in the vestry. Perhaps that encouraged the minister that I was more worldly minded than his flock. In any case, he soon drew me to one side and asked for my assistance in a delicate matter. He had, he said, placed a large bet on a certain horse at the local race-track, and was therefore concerned to help it win. For this he needed a black-magic potion from a medicine man. Please could I go and collect it?

By now the church membership cards were in such total chaos that I felt I could use a break. So the minister lent me his bicycle and I wobbled off (I'd not ridden before) to Borrowdale race-course. There a church elder who worked at the race-course and was also a medicine man in his spare time, gave me a package of horse urine, horse dung, and the footprint of a horse in some mud, among other things. 'Keep this safe,' he said. 'And whatever you do, don't look back once you leave here, or you will dilute the charm.'

As I cycled back I did some hard thinking. My knowledge of Presbyterianism was admittedly sketchy, but even I felt somehow that Presbyterians did not normally practise black magic. So why was this pastor doing so? When I saw how excited the pastor was with his horse urine, dung and footprint, I asked him about it.

He seemed exasperated by my stupidity. 'Of course I must have the potion: how else can I win? But you must not tell any of your friends, ever!'

'My friends?' What would the Black Shadows care about a horse's footprint?

'Yes – the elders of this church!'

'Oh.' I'd forgotten I had claimed 'friends' in such high

places. Soon after this the minister discovered what a mess I'd made of his church membership cards, and threw me out. This gave me an afternoon to lie in the sun and reach some conclusions about the Christian God. I decided that there was no power in this religion, as the minister himself went to the spirits for help. But the minister had not wanted his congregation to know he used black magic, so they must believe he asked the Christian God for help. He was deceiving them. Why? Somehow being a Presbyterian minister must give him power over them, while he himself knew there was no real power in this religion.

Then I remembered a time when my father had been friendly with some white Christian missionaries. They had invited us to visit them, and he had taken me, a very little boy, along. When we got to the missionaries, they would not let us go into their house or drink from their cups. They made us sit on the porch steps and gave us an old tin to drink from while they told us about their God and how we must obey him or die.

That reminded me of something the Nationalists at the NDP had been saying – that the missionaries had told the Africans to pray to the Christian God in order to get them to close their eyes so that the missionaries could steal the country from them.

At this point I sat straight up in the sunshine. For the first time in my life I felt a surge of real political anger go through me. My father and mother and I had been taken in by a hoax! All those times Papa preached at the church he was being used. There was nothing in it at all.

Of course, this was years later, and my parents long gone, but I sat there in the sun and felt furious. We had been used. To what end, I had no idea. Still, it made me angry and very suspicious of the Christian Presbyterian God. However, it also gave me an idea which I pursued with some success. From this time on, I began to attend the Highfield Presbyterian Church occasionally with two purposes in mind: to talk to the pretty girls in the choir, and to steal money from the collection plates for my drink and occasional drugs. I figured that if the Presbyterian pastors were cheating their congregations for profit, why shouldn't I?

The second incident happened shortly afterwards. One day in town I met a white lady whom I recognised as having played tennis at the tennis club. To my astonishment, she offered me work as a houseboy at her palatial home in Southerton suburb. She explained that her houseboy had left without warning, and she was desperate.

I jumped at it – recalling those years when, as a ragged child, I had thought that working for a white person was the pinnacle of success. This would be wonderful!

Mrs Smith, as I shall call her, soon realised she had a raw recruit on her hands. While I stared in wonder around her luxurious bungalow, she demonstrated how to iron a shirt, how to scrub a floor. Unfortunately, our standards differed. I had never been concerned about wrinkled clothes in my life, and as long as I got some wrinkles out of her clothes, I could not see why she got upset that there were others left in – or indeed even added by me. Another slight hitch was that when I ironed the shirts for her husband and sons, I would be tidy and button the cuff buttons. They would plunge their arms into the shirts in a hurry, and pop the buttons off every time. This infuriated them, but I kept forgetting not to do it.

It was the same with scrubbing floors. The only homes I'd ever known had had dirt floors. So when she led me out to the dazzling white-tiled floor in her kitchen and said I must get the dirt off, I couldn't even see where the dirt was. Dirt to me was lying up to my neck in a hole in the sand in the rain. Not a faint grey smudge here and there on a dry, otherwise immaculate floor.

Nevertheless, I was trying. She said: very trying. Her exasperation soon showed: 'You black kaffirs! You are baboons, you know that? Darwin proved it. You used to live in trees.'

As far as I knew I had not personally met this Mr Darwin, and I did not know if he had proved it or not, but I resented the very idea of a white man running around Salisbury saying the blacks came from baboons. Yet it also concerned me. White people were so smart. Perhaps this Darwin was right. Was he likely to come to this house and tell me that I came from a baboon? What would I do if he did?

'We whites, we come from God!' added Mrs Smith as she left me on my hands and knees on her kitchen floor.

Pay was little, and her moans were constant. Within days I'd had enough of white people. They obviously hated us blacks, and what was worse, laughed at us and treated us with contempt. I could not laugh at Mrs Smith, or treat her with contempt, as she was obviously rich and smart, so the only thing left to me was hatred. I ran away, leaving doors and windows open. I hoped she'd be burgled.

My friends were not sympathetic to my grumbles about the church and the whites. 'What did we tell you?'

'Don't be a chicken, Stephen! You are a doormat of the white man. They'd use your back to stand their shoes on.'

I thought of Mrs Smith, and for the second time I could feel real political anger. The Nationalists were right – it was time to get rid of the whites and claim our country for ourselves.

'Come to the secret liberation meetings going on in Highfield.'

So I went, and I kept on going. When my friends left to

join a Nationalist-run briefing hide-out held secretly in the rocky bush on the outskirts of Highfield, I went with them. The briefing hide-out was a natural cave in the rocky crevices. Ten of us could squeeze into it at a time – more than enough for any one meeting, because we did not want to draw attention to ourselves. Once inside, we would listen to our local leader in the nationalist cause. He blamed our poverty and frustration on the whites, and told us that without our willingness to fight, we would never be free. This was one of many such camps where young black men would go for briefing by the Youth League leaders. They would advise us on how to cause civil unrest and trouble, and then send us back into the townships.

Belonging to the Youth League gave me the novel delight of actually feeling *wanted* by somebody. At last I was made to feel I was good for something. The Youth League leaders accepted me for what I was. Nobody attacked or mocked me because I was poor, black and illiterate. Indeed, we were told we had rights and that it was time we seized them.

The training camp soon became an extended family for me, and also for the other lads. It was the only grouping I'd ever known – apart from us Black Shadows – which had not treated me with contempt. Thus I was ripe to accept the history of Africa as seen through Marxist-trained eyes. Our teachers kept it very simple for young men like us, and the main gist was roughly as follows:

Once upon a time all the blacks in Africa were good and happy and owned their land. Then the whites came. They saw the richness of the land and they wanted it for themselves. So they sent the missionaries to take it from us. The missionaries came with guns and Bibles. They read from the Bible and used it to deceive us. They told us to kneel and pray to their white God, and while our eyes were closed they took our land and treasures. By the time we opened our eyes it was too late: they had guns to kill us.

As proof of this version of history, they produced a picture of a statue of David Livingstone complete with gun and Bible. We all nodded soberly. There you were – a picture could not lie. We laughed at people who'd always thought that the gun had been to kill animals.

I was in my late teens, and it was the very first history lesson I had ever had, given to me by the very first people who had ever been kind to me. I felt that at last I had discovered the real truth behind all the misery of my life so far. All right, I would now hate all whites, all missionaries and anything to do with the Bible.

Next our teachers brought the story up to date. They reminded us of the poverty of our lives, and contrasted this with the opulence of the whites, with their big cars, vast homes, years of education and beautiful belongings.

'All that is yours. It is yours by right. Are you just going to sit there and let the white man have your things while you starve?' The thought of this inflamed us. Our leaders did not have to work hard to persuade desperately poor black teenagers that it was unfair that the whites should always have the best of everything.

So what was the solution? Nationalism, said our leaders. Only when the country had become nationalist-run by the blacks could we expect social justice and fair play. They sketched a marvellous future for us once the revolution had come, and all things were held in common: we were reminded of all the big cars the whites had, always carefully locked.

'When our day comes, cars will be left with keys inside the ignition. You'll be able to hop in any of them and drive away. All things will be available for everyone.'

I thought of a certain white Mercedes I'd always

admired at the golf club. I thought of its white owner conveniently shot, and that car there for me to drive away. I liked the idea very much. As for houses, wow! 'You will be able to live in any one you like!' Oh my – no more sleeping under bridges! I decided to take Mrs Smith's house when the day came. Serve her right.

The idea impressed on us again and again was: you are treated as slaves in your own country. What right do white people have to do this to you? What are you going to do to stop them? If you don't, they will steal everything from you.

What exactly we were going to do to stop white people was the next part of the course: training in combat, sabotage and ways to create civil unrest. I learned how to use small arms and petrol bombs. Sometimes I thought back to all those American films of the Wild West I'd seen. My dreams had come true – at last I knew how to shoot people. I felt the excitement of power as I thought of shooting for the good of my country.

We fledgling Youth League members were instructed in the best methods of civil disruption and fear – how to start riots, and prepare and throw petrol bombs in public places. All the methods had one aim in common – not so much to kill a few dozen or even a few hundred people here and there, but to create terror among thousands and thus undermine the government and law of Rhodesia.

Our training was not for the faint-hearted. The discipline was strict. We were sometimes starved to get us used to accepting hardship in the line of duty. They told us that we would soon be the real rulers of our country. Together we would destroy the whites and capitalism and Christianity and everything else the whites stood for. Each of us would be used in the way that seemed best.

This led to great grief and frustration on my part. Several

of my friends in the camp could read and write, and they were destined for further training and higher command. But not me. What could be done with an illiterate, ignorant teenager like me? My bitterness at this rejection tasted sour in my mouth. I could hardly blame my new leaders. Here it was again – my past abandonment by my parents was poisoning my whole life.

The hatred and self-pity rose like bile within me. I'd never had any kind of chance in life. But our trainers were wise. Their pep talk channelled my frustration into a desire for revenge on those whom I felt had let me down – the church (were not my parents church folk?), and the whites (whose garbage I had sifted through for years).

'You can still do great things for the cause in the township, Stephen. Stay near your township and cause trouble. We need you to help start riots.'

So by 1960 I was a fully primed member of the Nationalist Youth League working for the liberation of Zimbabwe. Or, as the government would have called me, a Marxist thug who should be shot for treason. By then I would have given my life for the liberation of Zimbabwe. I believed absolutely that the revolution would solve all my problems and make me happy.

So the months went by. As long as I was with the Black Shadows, I could forget my problems and join in their Youth League activities. We had a busy time of it. We threw petrol bombs into parks and beer gardens (these were government funded and run and gave the whites a good revenue). We attacked churches, police cars and open-air gatherings – most memorably one at the Cyril Jennings Hall in Highfield, at which the Prime Minister, Edgar Whitehead, was due to speak. We started riots by joining any unhappy gathering in the townships and stirring the people to violence and demonstration.

Belonging to this tight-knit group gave me plenty of companions, but as the months went by somehow very little companionship. Everyone seemed so full of anger and hate. I didn't blame them: I was angry too. Deep inside I knew I was nowhere near the happiness that the revolution had promised me. I would feel desperately unhappy at times, but tell myself to be patient – the revolution had not yet fully come. Wait until I had the house and the car . . . .

But I could not be with the Black Shadows all the time, and when I was alone, a great emptiness and depression would come over me. I felt so alone, so desolate

Then one Sunday morning in May 1962, when I was nearly twenty years old, there was a combined political rally of the NDP, the UNIP of Zambia, and the Malawi Congress Party held in the grounds of the Cyril Jennings Hall in old Highfield. The excitement raised the political temperature for miles around. Thousands of workers decided to stage the mother of all strikes for the entire following week. The country would be plunged into turmoil. We members in the Youth League wanted to get in on the action, and decided to attack anyone who was trying to break the strike and go to work anyway.

But that was for the Monday, and we were eager to do something right away on that Sunday, the same day as the rally. And so one of us came up with the bright idea of going into Machipisa Shopping Centre that evening and throwing petrol bombs at the local bank.

The idea sounded fine to me. My friends and I spent the afternoon in the mouth of a cave well hidden from police and prying eyes, filling the bottles with petrol and wicks, assembling our knives. It was a leisurely occupation, helped by beer and lazing about in the sun, looking forward to the night's excitement.

CHAPTER SIX

THE TENT MEETING

We left our hide-out at about 6 pm, as darkness fell, and
began walking towards Machipisa. In a field near the
township, on the premises of the then Dutch Reformed
Church, we saw something that had certainly not been
there a few days before when we last came this way: a
vast, billowy tent.

Obviously some meeting was about to begin, because
there were many people in the tent and still more going
inside. A few cars were parked outside. The tent was
packed and we could hear music. People were singing.

'What is that, eh?' my friend Edson wondered aloud.

'A circus?' I hazarded hopefully. Any entertainment was
always welcome to me. A few seconds later a piano accordion sounded somewhere deep in the tent. We paused.
Soon the notes gathered themselves together and shakily
became a song.

A chorus. A chorus! No self-respecting circus would
have a chorus. My goodness, it was some sort of Christian
meeting. We lads, pausing in the dusty road, needed only a
quick confirmation of glances to agree that this phenome-
non needed investigating. We hurried closer to the tent.

'Dorothea Mission' said a small banner on the side of the tent.

'Oh, it's the Dorothea Mission,' said Edson, who liked to show off that he could read.

'So who are they?'

'They are . . . ah . . . a mission.'

'And?'

'I don't know. It just says, "Dorothea Mission",' he shrugged.

'Great.' I gave him what I hoped was a withering look. I could not read, and was very sensitive on the subject.

'Dorothea Mission' conveyed precisely nothing to any of us. But by now we were among the throng of people, and so more information was easily acquired.

'The Dorothea Mission?' A lady paused at our question. 'They are Christians from South Africa. Come to the meeting and hear them.' And she hurried on.

South African Christians! My, oh my! I was galvanised. It would have been a crime to leave it alone. I turned to my gang. 'Hey, nothing good comes from South Africa. It is full of segregation and apartheid. Why should such people come here to Rhodesia to preach about their god? They've really come to brainwash us black people, to make us too soft to fight for our freedom.'

They nodded angrily, and a plan began to form. Hastily I continued: 'These Christians, they need a lesson. Tonight we'll give it to them – let's blow them up!'

It didn't take much of an imagination to foresee that some well-aimed petrol bombs thrown into the tent would produce panic and damage well worth seeing. It would be far more satisfying than attacking the impersonal concrete walls of a bank. It would give us a sense of power and prove that we could make things happen – we would make our mark. It was an opportunity for feeding our hate on a hitherto unimagined scale.

Quickly I worked out a simple plan, and divided my twelve friends into pairs. I would get them to surround the tent. No one would suspect the lads wandering about at the entrance. They would mingle with all the other curious passers-by.

Now to co-ordinate our attack. This was the biggest thing I had ever planned, and I wanted it done in style. I decided that we were to attack at 7 pm.

'At 7 pm I will whistle and everybody throw their stones and petrol bombs into the tent entrance,' I said. They grinned in anticipation. 'I want,' I continued, 'everyone inside that tent to die.'

'Fine,' said the Black Shadows.

Of course this was impossible, given our limited weapons, but my friends shared my hatred of Christianity, and were as inflamed as me by that morning's political rally. Their eyes gleamed with excitement. I liked the feeling of power and I did not think twice about the terror and injuries I was intending to inflict. I, Stephen Lungu, was planning to attack a tent with many hundreds of people inside. None of the other Youth League members in our area had done that yet. It would help my reputation like nothing else.

'Remember,' I warned, 'everyone inside the tent must die. If you allow anyone to escape, I'll give you the gift of a bullet!' This sounded great to me, and I certainly meant it at that moment. I was a violent, vicious, emotionally damaged young man.

After whispered consultation as to what we would do afterwards, and an agreement to meet up eventually in the shopping centre, George suddenly pointed out: 'But it is only five minutes to seven. We still have five minutes.'

'Five minutes? Right, then let's go in and see what's

going on,' I suggested. 'We'll stay for only two minutes.'

Little did I realise what those two minutes were going to cost me.

And so the twelve of us entered the tent, and found the bench at the very back free, almost as if it had been kept empty for us. We sat down in a row and looked about us. Many of the common folk of Highfield township had come along, thin men in shabby shirts and trousers, and women magnificent in floral dresses. We admired the pretty girls who had also turned out.

They were still singing choruses, and we twelve laughingly joined in – singing deliberately off key to annoy people. It worked. A Zambian preacher (as I later learned he was) acting that night as a steward, approached me and laid a restraining hand upon my shoulder. 'Please don't sing like that,' he remonstrated.

I hated being touched. I turned on him and pulled my knife. 'Get off! If you touch me again, I will kill you,' I snarled.

He backed away in some confusion.

Then the singing of choruses suddenly stopped. The two minutes were up and we were about to leave when a man stood up on the platform at the middle of the tent. He said, 'We have a girl here whose life has been changed, even on the streets of Soweto. She will now share her testimony as to how Jesus came into her life. Her name is Rebecca Mpongose.'

A girl? *Preaching?* We were astonished, and sat in confusion. A woman addressing a major tent meeting was unheard of!

I was amazed, and craned my neck for a good look. A lovely young woman approached the microphone and began to speak. 'I am Rebecca Mpongose from Soweto in South Africa,' she began politely.

For a moment I was too flabbergasted to hear another thing she was saying. I had never seen a woman 'preach' in my life, and to have such a beautiful young woman talking to such pathetic people as *Christians* seemed a crime against nature. Never in my wildest dreams had I ever thought good-looking women had anything to do with Christianity. Surely only old grannies or ugly girls with flat noses were Christians. Pretty women, I strongly felt, should walk majestically in the streets for us men to admire. Rebecca's beauty was wasted here!

But I couldn't deny her radiance, and at this point I was so curious that I began to listen. She was talking about some friend of hers, Jesus, and how when she had found him, her life had really begun – his love had transformed everything. There was a strange uncanny authority and resonance with which she spoke of forgiveness and a new start in life, and I suddenly felt very dirty and shabby.

I leaned forward, entranced by her and the joy she had. It was so obviously real that it moved me deeply and I yearned for it. 'Who has she found? *Jesus?*' I had heard the name years ago in the Presbyterian church, but it had not meant anything to me. Christianity for me meant God. Then I pulled myself up short.

For an African man to be moved or persuaded by a woman to do anything was unthinkable. But I had been deeply moved by Rebecca and her talk of Jesus, and this shook me considerably. However, I did not dare think of really responding to her invitation to come to Jesus, because I was with my gang, and they would think I was a sissy.

The gang was getting restless. 'Let's go,' Edson whispered. But an indescribable longing, a yearning for something, was sweeping over me. I realised I had just seen someone who had found something truly wonderful. I had never imagined religion could be like this. Witchcraft and ancestors' spirits produced a very different effect on people.

'Another two minutes, please!' I whispered impatiently, and pulled Edson back down beside me. I didn't feel embarrassed to ask him for more time, as we were all admiring such a beautiful girl. The gang need not know that as well as fancying her, I also wanted to hear how her life had actually been changed.

My friends rolled their eyes in exasperation as they settled uneasily on the bench. I turned back to listen to the girl, but she was just finishing.

'I want you to listen to what this man, Shadrach Maloka, an evangelist from South Africa, has to say.' She gave another blinding smile and stepped to one side as a tall black man in his early thirties walked across to the front of the platform.

This would have been the natural point for me to turn away and give the signal. After all, it was now well past seven. But still I paused, ignoring my group's growing irritation. The charm of the girl lingered, and I was momentarily curious to hear if this preacher would say anything about this Jesus who could command such devotion from such a beautiful girl. I suppose that I expected the man to radiate the same joy.

Not a bit of it.

Slowly this Shadrach Maloka stepped up to the microphone and gazed out over the packed throng. He had a commanding presence and poise. But he simply stared at us. And all of us there in that crowded tent stared back. Slowly a total silence fell on the crowd. It was uncanny. Then without any warning he thundered:

'Romans 6:23 says, "The wages of sin is death. But the gift of God is eternal life in Christ Jesus our Lord." And 2

Corinthians 8:9 says, "For you know the grace of our Lord Jesus Christ, that though he was rich, yet for your sakes he became poor, so that you through his poverty might become rich."'

I jumped, as did many people. 'What a rude guy,' I thought indignantly. 'Not so much as a hello.'

I was about to turn away and give my signal when I realised that the preacher had become silent again. His eyes searched the crowd like moral spotlights, but he did not say another word.

Utter silence. Nothing. He stood motionless. I could not believe this and gaped at the man. In the quiet his first words still rang in my head: 'The wages of sin is death.'

Sin is death!

Sin is death!

Sin is death!

The silence seemed to echo with the phrase. Seconds piled up into several minutes. He was simply standing there staring at us, but he certainly had the electrified attention of the crowd. Sin is death!

Through my mind flashed all the evil things I had done of late, all the hatred I had shown. Death, death. No one had to tell me I was going to die as I had lived: in evil and misery. My mind flashed back to my family: how I hated my father and mother and aunts. My mind flashed forward to my present lifestyle of violence and robbery and hatred of everyone outside my gang.

And then, this man's face began to crumple up. His great dark eyes filled with tears. They ran down his cheeks. Harsh sobs racked him. He was crying! Well, I was astounded. I'd been prepared for ranting and raving, and would have shut my mind to it. But nothing had prepared me for this.

Chills galloped in little groups up and down my spine.

'This is . . . another thing again!' I whispered to my friend. I could not have moved now if I'd wanted to. First the beautiful girl, and then this. Why was this obviously powerful preacher crying? I'd never seen such a thing. I was mystified.

And then at last the man began to speak again. Slowly. Solemnly. Every eye in the tent was fixed on him.

'I am crying. I am crying because the Holy Spirit has told me that many people here tonight may die without Christ.'

I remembered my reason for being there with a jolt that had the force of an electric shock. I was here to cause chaos, and this preacher was saying he knew about our plan! I gasped. *How* did he know about our gang and its petrol bombs? I nearly dropped the paper bag with the bottles of petrol I was holding with the shock of it. Meanwhile, the preacher was speaking again. 'Many of you are in grave danger,' he thundered. 'These are violent times. You may die soon.' He repeated it several times.

His utter assurance could only mean one thing – someone must have warned him about me. But how? We ourselves had only just decided. I felt rising panic. If he knew our plan, his stewards would know who we were. Anyway, there was obviously no time to be lost.

'Get ready,' I whispered, frightened that even now the stewards in the tent were edging towards us. I fumbled in my bag to prepare my home-made petrol bombs. I was ready now, and about to tell my gang to get out quick.

But the preacher was talking again. 'If you work for one company, you get your wages from that company. You can't get it from another. If you work for the devil, you will get his wages: death.

'And all of you deserve the wages of the devil – death!' Suddenly Shadrach Maloka's voice turned to a booming threat. He jabbed at the crowd with an accusing finger. 'For all of you have sinned. You have cheated. You have lied. You have harmed people.'

Jab, jab, jab went that finger. I flinched and thought of the people I had attacked. It seemed that the preacher was pointing directly at me, as if he knew every bad thing I had ever done. I was appalled, and embarrassed in front of my friends. I tried to defend myself in an angry whisper, 'This preacher has no manners at all. Why does he point so?' Edson gave me a stare of total incomprehension.

But the preacher continued: 'You have disobeyed God, and you think he does not see your evil lives? Even every time you open your mouth, you sin. Your language is full of blasphemy and deceit. Your tongues are as full of poison as vipers.'

I was stunned. Only the previous day Robert's primus stove would not light. I had kicked it violently, and sworn at it, sending it to hell several times over. But how did this man know?

I could think of only one way. Robert, sitting near me on the bench, must have told him. So I pulled out my knife and whispered to him savagely. 'How dare you tell this man my sins? I will kill you!'

Robert jumped and stared at me in total amazement. Obviously, though, he was feeling guilty as well, because he said, 'Well, you've told him about me as well, so I will kill you too!'

We glared angrily at each other, but meanwhile the preacher carried on talking about sin and the damage it did. He kept on pointing, and the more he spoke, the more I felt he was talking directly to me.

I know now that I, Stephen Lungu, had without warning hit a spiritual crisis in my life. But at the time I didn't know I had a spirit, and I did not in the least understand what was happening to me. I was a very simple, literal person, with no sophistication whatever, and to me it was as if that preacher was standing up there talking only about me, and telling everyone the secrets of my heart. I had not realised then that people's hearts are very much the same.

By now our planned attack was quite forgotten. The preacher's pointing finger had me mesmerised. But I never dreamed of just leaving the tent. Instead, I decided to be clever, and in my very simple, literal way, avoid his finger by ducking down every time he pointed. Soon I was bobbing up and down like a duck, and trying Edson's patience to the utmost. My bag of home-made petrol bombs bounced about alarmingly.

It was a strange way in which to hold the greatest spiritual crisis of my life, shying about at the back of a dusty tent, armed with deadly weapons, but frightened stiff of the accusing finger of an unarmed preacher.

Then, quite suddenly, the preacher shifted his ground yet again. He was speaking now of Jesus, in tones of warmth and compassion. This Jesus, it seemed, had lived long ago and had seen a thing or two. He was not a big ruler, but poor and powerless and from an oppressed race, like us. He had had no home and no money, and nobody really understood him. But he had had tremendous power all the same, and knew the secret of life, and healed people who were sick, and helped them. He had finished by being murdered by those whom he had come to save, and because of his death, he had made peace with God for us. Because of him, any one of us could have eternal life with him.

The preacher then repeated 2 Corinthians 8:9 – 'For you know the grace of our Lord Jesus Christ, that though he was rich, yet for your sakes he became poor, so that you through his poverty might become rich.' Suddenly I began to understand what Christianity was all about. It was for someone like me! I could identify with this Jesus. He had suffered in all the ways that I knew so well. Poverty, oppression, hunger, thirst, loneliness. I had known all of these, and so had he. But the amazing thing was, he had not needed to know such suffering – but he had accepted it in his love for me. He had come to earth for my sake, to pay the price for my sins. My wages were death, but Jesus paid the price for me. On the cross he had become a nobody that I could become a somebody.

The preacher was now saying that anyone who wanted could have this Jesus. I could exchange my poverty and sin for Jesus' love and riches. The transaction that Jesus was offering me suddenly became clear. Then I stopped bobbing about and sat still, utterly at an end to myself. Tears for all the pain, loneliness, self-hatred and fear I had known coursed down my cheeks. If this great burden could not be removed by this Jesus, I no longer wanted to live.

Now Africans are wonderfully tolerant of self-expression but there is a limit. People in the crowd began to turn and stare curiously at me as I sat there sobbing. This was too much for the rest of my gang. They began to get very restless. But I was beyond caring about what they thought.

I wanted nothing in the world but to be delivered of this intolerable burden of pain and hurt and evil that haunted me.

So clutching my bag of petrol bombs, I stumbled through the little group of people around me and began to make my way forward. I had never been to a service like this, and I had no idea that the preacher intended to invite people forward at the end of the service in any case. I simply wanted to be near him. He would help me find this Jesus.

It seemed to me that the other people in the tent must understand this – that I just wanted to cry with the preacher. The tension and strain of years were tearing me apart now. The misery and fear of the little lost child resurfaced; inside

I was still screaming for love and security.

I'd never heard of 'repentance' and 'forgiveness'. The preacher simply said it was possible to exchange my poverty for Jesus' riches, and this was what I wanted. The preacher's eyes flickered when he saw me coming forward, but he was in his stride now, and simply preached on. A moment later I reached the front. My knees simply gave out, and I slumped down in front of him. His words washed over me in a torrent I barely understood. I just knew that he held the promise of relief, of succour from the waves of pain. I reached out and held onto his feet. (I learned later that my gang thought at that moment that I was about to attack and kill the preacher!)

Then strong arms grabbed at me, trying to wrench me away. The stewards had arrived, and obviously felt that a sobbing young man clutching at the preacher was not a good thing. But I had nowhere else in the world to go, and so I clung like a limpet. My howls intensified.

Now this preacher was one determined man, but even he was distracted by the crowd that was rapidly becoming a bit of a scrum at his feet. He was, after all, trying to address a rally of many hundreds of people, and our heaving shoulders and flailing arms kept disrupting his line of vision. He finally paused in what he had to say and glared at his stewards.

'Leave the lad alone!' he commanded. 'You are disturbing me!' In his eyes there was no room for opposition.

Embarrassed, the stewards fell back. With a brief glance down at me, crying and crushed at his feet, Shadrach Maloka took a deep breath – and continued preaching!

A moment later an avalanche of stones flew into the tent. People screamed in panic, and chaos broke out.

CHAPTER SEVEN

THE PETROL BOMB

A minor explosion followed as a petrol bomb was flung onto the outside canvas of the tent, setting it ablaze. Little sheets of flame sprang up, but fortunately did not spread. People screamed. A moment later dozens of stones were hurled against the tent, and many of them came inside, injuring some people. I turned in horror. Had my friends gone ahead without me? I'd forgotten all about them.

There was a heavy stampede out of the tent. People were knocked over and risked being crushed under foot. Mothers shielded their babies. There were screams inside and shouts outside. I learned later that the political tension whipped up in that morning's political rally had exploded, and violence had broken out across the whole township that night. Everywhere young black men were demonstrating their fury and rebellion against the white government. Highfield always spelt big trouble for the government, and would do so for years to come, with many of the country's major black nationalist leaders being residents of Highfield.

The preacher still stood on the platform. Trembling, I knelt beside him. Nearby, the members of the Dorothea

Mission gathered by the platform, and quietly began to sing. They chose the chorus 'There is power, power, wonder-working power in the blood of the Lamb'. It sounded peaceful and soothing compared to all the commotion outside.

I glanced at the preacher. His face was drawn, but composed. He closed his eyes and I realised that he was praying. That reminded me of what he'd said at the beginning of his talk: that he was crying because many here might die tonight. How had he known of the danger? Who had warned him?

More shouts and trampling feet followed. The preacher and I were trapped at the eye of a hurricane of violence. A few minutes later we could hear the rushing of many vehicles. We learned later that the government had sent in their riot squad to quell the trouble that was engulfing Highfield that night. Outside looked like a vision of hell. There were obviously hundreds of violent protestors out there. I learned later that the Dorothea Mission tent was only one of many dozens of targets that night.

The leaders of the Dorothea Mission team were concerned for the safety of the people who had left the tent and run into all the trouble outside. They tried to reach the entrance of the tent, and shout for them to come back inside, but the hail of stones kept them away.

By now there were just a very few people left inside the tent with the Dorothea Mission team. To comfort them, the Mission leaders began to sing another chorus. The golden sound fell like a sweet shower in a hissing bedlam. Then the team members prayed, asking for God's protection from the trouble outside.

The preacher was suddenly aware of me. His dark eyes, so full of grief at the trouble outside, focused sadly on me. 'Young man, what can I do for you?' he asked gently.

I looked round me. Everywhere fear and violence, and yet here in the tent, calm voices sang and prayed to Jesus. It was an illustration of my whole existence. In the midst of my frenzied hate, I had stumbled across an oasis of love and peace. I wanted it, I wanted Jesus.

So I asked the preacher: 'Can your Jesus save even someone like me?'

'Yes,' he said. 'Jesus died for you. God loves you.'

God loved me! Why bring him into it? What had God ever done for me? He had left me to nearly starve. I felt angry with God, and so I reacted in my usual headstrong fashion: 'Preacher, you tell me that God loves me, and I will kill you right now.' I fumbled for my knife. 'I don't want to hear about God, but I want you to tell me about Jesus.'

The preacher blinked and then looked me over with grave consideration. My little bag of petrol bombs was taken into account. Then he said gently, 'Young man, suppose you tell me about yourself first, and why you want this Jesus.'

So I began to tell him about me. At first it came out in ragged bits and then, as I felt less self-conscious, I poured out my story, with all the pain and hurt. It was the first time anyone had ever asked me about myself – and ever wanted to hear.

I told about my unhappy family. My father's hatred and rejection of me, the break-up of my parents and the awful day when my mother had abandoned me as a child. I relived the panic and total desperation I had felt. The pain of feeling that everyone in the world who knew me hated me, that there was no one to turn to.

To my astonishment, the preacher began to cry along with me. 'Why are you crying?' I wondered to myself. He continued to weep as I told of my nights under the bridge, my constant search for food in the stinking dustbins, my becoming a gang member, my fear of everything.

He looked at me with the strangest expression in his eyes. It was compassion. This really melted my heart. No one in my life had ever before cared at all for me. That this stranger should have enough feeling for me to cry for my misery was like the love of Christ shining down on me.

When at last I'd finished my story, he paused, and then said gently, 'Young man, I shall now tell you a story. Many years ago there was a fourteen-year-old girl who became pregnant. People asked her who was responsible, and she pointed out the young man. But he refused all responsibility. He did not want the child. After nine months the child was born. The girl did not want it either. Two weeks later she wrapped the baby in a towel and stuffed it into the toilet and ran away. A woman nearby heard little sounds. She investigated and found the baby drowning in the toilet. She rushed it to hospital and the child survived.

'Young man, I was that child. I never again saw my mother. I have no idea who she was. And I have no idea who my father was. Like you, neither of them ever wanted me.'

I stared at him in utter astonishment. This was not possible. This man bore all the signs of being loved and secure within himself. Where had this come from?

The preacher was turning over some pages in his Bible. 'I want to read something to you,' he said, 'that sums up people like you and me. It is a promise from God and his Son, Jesus Christ, to people like us. It is from Psalm 27:10: "Though my father and my mother forsake me, the Lord will take me up."'

The words rang in my head. 'The Lord will take me up. The Lord will take me up.' There it was: this man was loved by somebody – the Lord had taken him up.

'You see,' the man went on. 'God and Jesus are the same thing: Jesus is God's Son. Jesus was simply God on earth. God has promised: "When your father and mother forsake you, the Lord will take you up." The people who adopted me named me Mohaneo – rejected one. That is how I felt throughout my childhood. Rejected by everyone, especially my mother. But in 1947 when I found Jesus, I was given a new name, Shadrach, by the missionaries. Shadrach was a man in the Old Testament whom God saved out of great tribulation, when everyone else had forsaken him. And I have learned that Jesus does not reject me. The Lord has taken me up.'

Hearing this verse was the changing point of my life. I felt for the first time that love from God was not impossible, that it could make sense even in my life. Here was a faith big enough to embrace the reality of the pain I had known, and still offer a way out. No one was denying that I had indeed been rejected and had been in misery. But now God was saying to me: 'But I am here and I will take you up. I love you.'

I knelt to approach God for the first time in my life. I did not know quite how to say it, but for the first time I realised God loved me and was waiting for me.

'God,' I cried, 'I have nothing. I am nothing. I can't read. I can't write.' My total inadequacy choked me. 'My parents don't want me. Take me up, God, take me up. I'm sorry for the bad things I've done. Jesus, forgive me, and take me now.'

Immediately I felt as if a heavy burden had rolled off my back. There was a tremendous rush of relief and peace. I was astonished by the joy that flowed through me. Me – a thrown-away child among the millions of Africa, but Jesus had found me.

So intent had I been on my conversation with Shadrach

Maloka that I had nearly forgotten the troubles outside. Now, as my sobs subsided, I became conscious of a great deal of movement at the flap doors to the tent. Shadrach Maloka and I turned and saw that things were quieting down enough for us to leave the tent. Several of the stewards were eyeing Maloka anxiously, wanting to talk to him. I realised it was time for me to go.

'I must go,' I said. 'Many other people need you now.'

His dark eyes flashed me a grateful thanks for understanding. 'But I am concerned you may be attacked by the scoundrels or the riot squads.' His eye fell again on my bag of petrol bombs. 'Let me walk you to the edge of the field, and see you safely on your way.'

'No,' I said, 'it is kind of you, but your Mission people need you now. I will be safe, and anyway, I am ready to die.' My spiritual elation was such that at that moment I would have almost welcomed death as a way of meeting God sooner rather than later.

Shadrach Maloka squeezed my shoulder. 'Yes,' he said, 'you are ready to die. But for the first time also, you are ready to live. God bless you.' He turned away to his Dorothea Mission team members.

I didn't dare leave my bag of petrol bombs there, and so I scooped it up again. Then I hurriedly eased my way out of the tent and into the troubled night.

It was not a pretty sight. Everywhere people were shouting and running. Riot squad vehicles raced up and down the dusty roads with their floodlights piercing the darkness of the night. The dark bulky shapes of men in riot gear stalked about, determined to disperse any small group. They wanted to restore order to this most troubled and violent township.

I hesitated to get my bearings. Where in the middle of all this chaos was my gang? I stumbled about, calling their names softly. I did not want to attract any interest. A few hundred metres from the tent, I fell over someone stretched out on the grass. The head was thrown back, the eyes opened wide in shock. I knew this lad – he was one of my own gang!

'George! George!' I whispered urgently. 'Get up!' I reached out to urge him to his feet, and found a large knife embedded in his chest. 'George?' He was dead. I sank onto the grass beside him in shock. I had known him for years. We were close as our gang would have reckoned us close. Now he was dead.

That set me thinking. It suddenly dawned on me that if I had not gone forward when I did, I might very well be dead now too. But I felt so guilty somehow that I should have survived and not George. Why me?

Angry voices and approaching footsteps brought me out of my daze. I could all too easily be joining George in a permanent way down there on the grass if I stayed much longer. I had to get out here. There was no use in looking for any of the other members of my gang – they would have fled by now.

I lay still and quiet until the men – whoever they were, moved on. Sadly I ran my hand down George's face in a final farewell. Then cautiously I raised myself up, and crouching low made off.

As I ran I thought. The political rally of that morning seemed a very long time ago, but the emotions it had stirred were still affecting thousands of people throughout Highfield township. Where would all this violence and hatred end?

A good long way from the tent, I paused for breath, and tried to compose myself. I was terribly thirsty and dazed by the events of the past couple of hours. For a little while I wandered aimlessly on the outskirts of New Highfield, among the crowds who had been caught up in the commotion at the tent. I bought some fruit juice – several times over. Then suddenly I wanted to be alone. God had met with me that night. I could do nothing for any of my friends.

I had nowhere to go, for I dismissed the idea of returning to our gang's hide-out in rocks outside the township. Not only would it be highly dangerous, with police swarming about, but I wanted no more of that lifestyle. Then I thought of the local bridge – 'my bridge' I called it. Hastily I made my way there.

As I walked along, the great changes of the night swept over me again. I had found Jesus! I didn't know my New Testament then, but later I found a good description of what I found in Christ that night: 'Be of good cheer, I have overcome the world', and, 'The peace of God, which passes all understanding.' The loving presence of the Lord warmed me all the way back to my bridge.

Cheerfully I tramped up the steep slope and then crawled in under shelter. Tears of joyful release ran steadily down my cheeks as I dug my shallow trench – my grave, I always called it. Before I crawled into it, I knelt in the sand to pray, exulting in this extraordinary feeling of peace and security. I had never dreamed of anything like it.

Then I stretched myself out cheerfully in my shallow 'grave', pulled a bit of sacking over me for extra warmth, and carefully scooped the sand and earth back over me – working my way from my feet up my thighs and body. I covered my left shoulder snugly enough, but as usual, found it impossible to cover my right arm very well. Flicking the sand up at my right shoulder usually succeeded only in getting it firmly in my eye.

However, I snuggled down as best as I could. I looked up from under the arch of the bridge. Far, far above me, thousands of stars glittered like tiny diamonds tossed in handfuls across a great soft black velvet cloth. How beautiful they were! It suddenly hit me that I had never admired them before. But no longer did they seem threatening or impassive to my suffering. 'God,' I whispered, 'why couldn't I see the beautiful stars before?'

I lay and thought about my life. I had so little to bring to God. I thought I'd better mention this to him again so that both of us would understand where we stood from the start.

'God,' I whispered. It felt wonderful to have someone to talk to. 'I've never really been to school. I can't read. I can't even write my name. But I want to spend the rest of my life telling people about you.' I couldn't imagine a more satisfying future. I literally ached to do it. I did not then know that the word 'evangelist' existed, but that would have summed up my new, blazing ambition. Meeting Jesus that night had been like waking up for the first time in my life. I longed for everyone to find him. However, it seemed impossible that anyone would ever listen to a thing I said. I thought about this. What good was enthusiasm if you had no skills? I started to weep. But gradually the tears grew less, and the indescribable peace remained. The fear had gone. I finally dozed off.

CHAPTER EIGHT

THE POLICE

I woke just before dawn. No one in Africa who sleeps out of doors and is not dead drunk or simply dead finds it easy to sleep later: our birds gather for a daily dawn rendering of the Hallelujah chorus. This morning I felt like joining in with their chirpy greeting of a new day. I wriggled out of my trench, brushed off the sand as best I could, and looked back in marvel at the events of the previous night. My first prayer this morning was pretty basic and direct: 'Are you still there, Lord?'

A loving conscious presence that was certainly new in my experience assured me that yes, he was. I was staggered. He must have been with me all the time I was asleep. My first night not alone. It brought tears to my eyes.

I didn't know then that what had happened to me was what the New Testament describes as being 'born again'. But that is exactly how it was for me. I felt an entirely new creation. All the old life and fear had passed away and for me all things had become new. I was aware of God as I never would have imagined only twenty-four hours ago – when I was collecting bottles for petrol bombs. The only way I can explain it is to say that when you are dead you don't know you are dead, and when you are spiritually reborn, you are suddenly conscious of a whole new realm all about you.

Marvelling at this, I strolled out from the bridge and made my way to the river to wash some sand off my face. There was a tree nearby. As I passed it, I hesitated. I wanted to try and explain something to God, and this might be a way of making my feelings really clear.

So I walked over and put my arms tight around that tree. I then looked up at the sky. 'God,' I said. 'See me? See this? If you were here beside me like this tree, I would hug you like this.'

I gave the tree another big hug to demonstrate 'This is how much I love you.' And I rested my body and cheek lovingly against the tree, revelling in the unaccustomed peace in my soul.

A few hundred metres away some women came through the bush on their way to the river. Out of the corner of my eye I noticed them stop and watch me as I hugged the tree and talked out loud. A moment later they quietly made off in another direction, further upstream. I smiled to myself and wished I could have spoken to them about Jesus, when suddenly a voice in my head addressed me out of the blue.

'Stephen,' it said. 'Stand up.' Startled beyond measure, I leaped back from the tree, and looked about me. Was I going crazy? I was scared.

'Stephen,' the voice continued in my head. 'I will send you to the nations that you do not know.'

That was all. I bowed my head in awe. I did not doubt that Jesus had just spoken to me. I did not doubt that he would fulfil his promise and send me to the nations to tell them about him. I did not have the foggiest idea of how.

It didn't seem to matter.

I looked about me. My little bag still containing my knife and a stolen revolver I had acquired lay nearby. The revolver had been stolen by a friend of mine, and given to me as I was the leader of the Black Shadows. I wanted to throw them away, but I was afraid of who might find them. That gave me the first clue as to how to begin my new life.

I would go and surrender myself to the police.

So I rinsed my face, picked up my bag, walked the little distance to the bus-stop, and climbed aboard the next bus into town. It was early Monday morning, and the bus was crowded with glum commuters. The world over, it seems, going to work early on a Monday is a trying business.

In my new-found excitement I did not perhaps appreciate these Monday morning blues. I could not keep my joy to myself. I felt I was going to burst any minute. Suddenly I jumped to my feet. People looked up dully at this ragged, sand-stained young man. I took a deep breath and said in a loud voice, 'Ladies and gentlemen, do you know what happened to me last night?'

Heads the length of the bus swung round. Eyebrows went up. Smiles of faint derision and frowns of faint apprehension played on people's faces. This was all they needed to make their Monday morning melancholy complete: a madman aboard their bus.

So I hastened to reassure my captive audience that everything was all right because I had some really good news. 'I'll tell you what happened to me last night,' I shouted over the gasping engine. 'I found Jesus!'

Dead silence. Then: 'Hush!' scolded one big strong man indignantly. 'What do you think you are doing! We don't preach on Mondays!'

'But I . . .' The bus lurched to a stop in order to collect yet more passengers. The doors opened and sullen dark faces peered in, looking for a small space into which they might squeeze. In the momentary lull in engine noise, I turned eagerly to the man, and thus did not see another man a seat or two away stand up and approach me.

'Yes, but –,' I began again, when I was roughly seized from behind. 'Huh?' I gasped.

'It's MONDAY!' the man bellowed. 'NO preaching! This is the white man's god!' A hard thump in the lower back followed and I shot out of the door of the bus as if rocket-propelled – landing face first in the clouds of dust. I was too utterly amazed to protest. As I spat grit out of my mouth, the bus gave a great roar and staggered off again. Several black faces pressed against the grimy windows and eyed me with mild interest.

I scrambled stiffly to my feet, feeling quite shaken. Preaching was obviously going to be more hazardous than I had anticipated. But where had I gone wrong? Never mind. I brushed myself off as best I could, and waited for the next bus. It finally arrived, and I climbed on. Meekly I stood in the crowded vehicle, and watched the glum, closed faces all about me. I had such joy, and they could have it too. If only they knew. . . .I felt the exhilaration of my new-found faith begin to sweep over me again, and the urge to tell them kept getting stronger and stronger. I tried, feebly, to resist. After all, one abrupt exit from a bus was enough for one day.

But soon I realised I was going to have say something or pop, so I edged my way along the bus until I stood beside the driver. He was wedged behind the large steering wheel, and was unlikely to be able to pitch me out without warning. My first lesson in evangelism had been learned – watch your back!

Also, I decided that this time I would tell just the driver –

at the top of my voice, so that others could overhear. So I began. If the bus driver was startled by the volume of my speech, he was also struggling too hard to keep the bus on the pot-holed road to spare a hand to shut me up.

'Good morning!' I bellowed.

'Good – good morning,' he stammered, looking up briefly in astonishment.

'I have something important to tell you. Last night my life was changed.'

'Huh?'

I was tensed for signs of hostility, but this time there was only continued astonishment as the driver glanced up at me.

'I found Jesus!' I blurted out.

The bus veered and headed straight for a ditch.

The driver struggled with it, and when he could reply, said nervously, 'Did you?'

Quickly I glanced behind me. People were staring at the ditch they had just missed, and hadn't thought of booting me out yet. So I carried on. With increasing ease, and volume, I told them of the tent meeting last night, and how I had gone by accident. People had heard of the riot, of course, and their attention was now truly caught. Throughout the bus people began to strain to hear. I raised my voice to a low shout – I was dying to tell everyone what had happened to me.

Soon, to my astonishment, some began to weep.

After that, as I paused for breath, one lady suddenly called out, 'What must we do to have this Jesus?'

Here I hit an unexpected hitch. I gaped at her. 'Well, you, you . . . ah. You . . . you.

'Yes?'

'Ah, I don't really know,' I stammered.

Several baffled, hurt looks greeted that. 'Well, it only

happened to me last night,' I apologised. I knew that I had found Jesus, but I hadn't the least idea of quite how it had happened, and how other people could find him.

By this time the bus had arrived in town. We passengers piled off. I followed, frustrated with my failure, eager to do something. To my amazement, a little group of them hesitated and then timidly approached me.

'Your Jesus has brought you so much happiness. What must we do?' one asked wistfully.

I could not leave them like this. So I hastily decided my course of action. What I would do was to introduce them to God and vice versa and let him take care of it. So I spoke firmly, 'Let's pray. Now.'

Eyes bulged in astonishment and the little group looked horrified. 'What, pray, here?' squeaked a woman, glancing at the morning hubbub at the bus-stop.

'Yes. Here, now.'

'In front . . . of people?' stammered another.

'Well, yes, why not?' I said. 'I did it last night. You can do it this morning. There is no problem. Let us kneel down.'

'Kneel! You want us to *kneel?!*' I may as well have suggested that they turn double somersaults.

'Yes, kneel!' I said firmly. 'If it means anything to you,' I said. 'Jesus died on a cross in public.' That much I remembered from last night. 'For your sake.'

So slowly, stiffly, and with great embarrassment, the little crowd sank to its knees. This brought us to the attention of the passers-by. And they were not amused – especially as they began to trip over us.

'What are you doing there?'

'Get up!'

'This is not a church!'

Scolding and jeers rained down on us. 'This is a street! You are hindering us!'

But I lifted up my voice and began to lead my little group in prayer. 'God,' I said, 'I've met these good people on the bus just now, and I told them about how I found your Son Jesus last night. They've said they would like to meet him too, because I've told them how he loves everyone in the whole world. So, here they are.'

I hesitated. I'd run out of prayer. But quiet murmurs and tears on the faces around me made me realise that I was not needed now anyway. So I just knelt there with them, quietly exulting in the joy and inexpressible privilege of having told people about Jesus. Nearly forty years later, I was still in touch with three of them – they became ministers of local churches.

A little while later I remembered I was on my way to give myself up to the police, so I gathered up my bag with the knife and stolen revolver, and leaving my new friends rejoicing in the dust, went on my way.

Finding the police station was easy. It was a great imposing building that had been a target of my resentment for several years now. This was also where I'd been brought twelve years before as a hysterical, abandoned child. But that was all over now and in the past. I'd been found. The Lord had taken me up.

I paused outside to hitch my bag firmly over my shoulder and then made my way in through the swing doors. There was a big reception area and a counter, and behind that several desks, at which sat policemen. The sight of them abashed me. What was I doing? But one had spotted me and came to the desk. My mouth was dry, my knees shaking, but I shambled timidly across the floor.

'Yes? What is it?'

I paused. How could I begin to explain myself? The surroundings gave me a clue. 'I am under arrest,' I said simply.

The policeman looked at me. He looked over my right shoulder and over my left shoulder. Then he looked over my head. Obviously something was missing. 'Where is the policeman who arrested you?'

'No policeman arrested me. I've been a member of the nationalist Youth League for several years now, and none of you caught up with me. But now the love of God, Jesus, has arrested my heart, and so I have come to surrender.'

The sergeant on duty gave me a look of mild alarm, as if to say, 'What kind of a nut have I got here?' So I produced my little bag and gently spilled the knife and the revolver onto the counter. He blinked and barked something to another policeman who quickly joined us.

All three of us stood and looked at the weapons. Carefully the second policeman said, 'What did you say happened to you?'

'The love of God arrested me last night,' I began again patiently. The policemen exchanged looks. Then the second one held up his hand. 'No, don't tell me, come with me.'

A few minutes later I was ushered into the office of a senior policeman. He was white! They brought my little bag in and set it down in front of him. They sat me down. He questioned me.

'Why have you come here?'

'The love of Jesus arrested me.'

'What do you mean?'

This was hard to put into words. 'Last night I became a Christian, and I realised that what I have been doing is wrong.'

'What have you been doing?'

'Bad things for the National Democratic Party.' There was a fine line here that I was not sophisticated enough to explain. I felt in my heart that the idea of black independence was not wrong, and I was by no means happy with the idea of whites ruling us for ever. But I wanted to renounce the violence, and indeed to leave politics to other people. I was just not a political animal.

'Where did you become a Christian?'

'At the Dorothea Mission's tent meeting last night.' Swift glances of recognition; they became angry. 'Did you throw bombs?'

'No. I *was* going to throw bombs, but I listened to the preacher and I found Jesus instead. I talked to the preacher about it. Then I poured my petrol away into the sand, and I've brought my knife and revolver to you.'

Assistants were called, and told to find this preacher. 'And while we are waiting, tell me more about the Youth League. Who do you work with?'

I paused. I should have expected this. I was being asked to betray my friends as evidence of my good faith. This was difficult. I wanted to surrender myself and take whatever punishment was coming, but I did not want to hurt my colleagues. 'They've been my friends.'

'Stephen, they are trained killers. People died last night. Would your God want that?'

'My friends did not do it.'

'They would have done if they'd got the chance. Stephen, they would kill Christians if they got the chance. Do you think your friends follow Jesus?'

No, I knew they did not. But I was still determined not to betray them. I realised in the hours of questioning that followed that in simply becoming a Christian I had become the enemy of my gang. So I told the police as much as they asked about me, but only very vague details as to my gang. To tell them more would have meant certain arrest for my friends, and murder for me when I returned to the streets.

Everything I said was taken down in writing, and followed up by more and more questions. The minutes stretched into hours. We went over and over certain points. Passwords, codes, details of future plots. I gave hardly any information away. 'I am not very high up,' I humbly and truthfully explained.

When the police finally finished with me that afternoon, they led me away to a small room and left me for a bit. I was tired but content. I was putting my life in order, but I had not betrayed anyone. I had confessed to stabbings, and other violence. They could throw away the key and just keep me here. Then the policeman returned and led me back to his boss. 'We have heard now from the Dorothea Mission,' he said. 'They vouch for what you have told us,' and he smiled at me for the first time. After that the tensions eased a great deal, and they looked at me with open curiosity. A penitent trouble-maker was new in their experience.

The senior policeman regarded me with almost rough kindness. 'Well, Stephen,' he said, 'if your Jesus has forgiven you, we forgive you also. There is nothing to be gained from keeping you here. You are free to go.'

Tears welled up in my eyes. I couldn't help it. I was very tired and I could hardly believe my ears. I gave the man a great shy smile. I felt dizzy. Heaven had forgiven me. The police now forgave me. I wiped my sleeve across my eyes and heaved a sigh of relief. I felt a bit dazed. Walls of hatred built for years had disappeared. I was at peace now with old enemies.

I bowed my head and nodded respectfully to everyone as they showed me to the door and I prepared to leave. Then I heard a firm tread behind me. 'Stephen.' It was the commissioner again.

I felt a sudden dread. Were they going to send me away

after all? I turned in some dismay. The commissioner came up to me at the entrance of the station and eyed me thoughtfully for a moment. Then he held out his hand 'Here is some money – go and buy yourself a Bible.'

'Sir!' I was astounded. 'Yes sir. I will, sir.' He smiled briefly. I carefully pocketed the money and set out from that police station on the next stage of my new life: the search for a Bible. I could not read a word, but that was a small problem.

CHAPTER NINE

ON THE BUSES

Who sold Bibles? I had no idea. I'd heard that supermarkets sold everything, so I decided to go there.

'I want to buy a Bible,' I said breezily to the assistant. Here was my big moment.

She looked me over. 'We don't sell Bibles,' she said flatly, and turned away.

Oh.

Oh well. Nothing daunted, I was soon back out in the warm sunshine, strolling along the row of shops. Now which one of these would sell a Bible? I'd never actually held a Bible, of course, but I had seen those belonging to other people, and so I knew what they looked like. They were black and made of leather. Well, shoes were black and made of leather. So I tried the next shoe shop I came to.

'I would like to buy a Bible,' I said.

The shop assistant looked me over. 'We don't sell Bibles,' she said, and turned away.

Back outside on the pavement I paused for a moment, feeling baffled. If supermarkets and shoe shops did not sell Bibles, who did? I strolled along again more slowly, trying to puzzle it out. Then suddenly I caught a glimpse of a bookshop across the road. A bookshop! Of course. I rushed across the road, narrowly avoiding a car, and sprinted into the shop. The assistant looked up, startled. I drew a deep breath. 'I would like to buy a Bible,' I said.

'We don't sell Bibles,' she said promptly.

My jaw must have dropped open in dismay, for she then continued; 'For Bibles, you need to go to the local church bookshop.' And she gave me instructions on how to find it, a few minutes' walk away.

My fourth attempt. This time I wasn't taking anything for granted. I walked in and enquired meekly, 'Do you sell Bibles?'

'Oh yes, of course!' said a gentleman with a bright smile. I heaved a sigh of relief.

'Fantastic.'

He looked up at me curiously, but said only, 'Shall I show them to you?'

He led me to a whole shelf of Bibles. He helped me choose a large black hard-covered Bible in the Shona language, which was spoken by most of the people in my township.

Outside the shop, I slipped it reverently out of the bag. I held it in both hands to examine it. It was impressively substantial. I sniffed at it. What a wonderful smell! Freshly cut and bound paper. It smelt so clean, so right. A book like this was obviously holy. I sniffed and sniffed in rapture at this wonderful fragrance of new book until I felt dizzy. Then I carefully balanced my Bible in one hand, and gently opened it. I hadn't opened a book in something like twelve years, since my brief visit to school under Aunt M. I couldn't remember if books were very fragile or not. It would have broken my heart to rip or soil it. I gazed in awe at the snowy white pages, and turned a few with great care, admiring the pristine whiteness of the margins, and the neat regiments of lines that marched across the page, the battalions of verses.

The fact that I could not actually read a word of it, and did not even know whether I held it upside down or not, seemed only a secondary consideration. I owned a Bible! As long as I had it to carry about with me, I had tangible evidence of my new life as a Christian.

Carefully I put it back in its bag, and made my way to the bus-stop for the trip to the township. Once again, as I had that morning, I took the opportunity of speaking to my fellow passengers. Several listened with interest. When the bus dumped me back in the suburbs, I stood for a moment in the warm sunlight, savouring my happiness. I still felt conscious of God's loving presence, and was also amazed that because of him, I was having the first 'friendly' conversations with other people that I could remember.

In fact, I'd enjoyed my bus ride so much that the next day, on the spur of the moment, I hopped onto a bus and went back into town. I spent a happy morning riding the buses back and forth from the township to town, telling anyone who would listen what Jesus had done for me. In Africa strangers talk to each other much more easily than in Europe or America, and there was no embarrassment at the fact that I spoke to them – just a mixture of reactions as to what I said. I could soon spot the pious church-goers. They'd say, 'Amen, Amen!' when they realised I was 'preaching'. The more 'respectable' church-goers had had enough on Sunday and were consistently of the opinion, 'No preaching during the week.' Then there were those who were very antagonistic to my talk of the whites' religion. I had to be careful with such people, as they got very angry. Finally, there were those who greeted what I had to say with real interest. This gave me such joy.

Back in Highfield that afternoon, I drifted towards the

place where the tent meeting had been held, and was told that the meetings were continuing, both here and at another place twelve kilometres away at what is now Mbare township. The Dorothea Mission announced that anyone who'd become a Christian was invited to a week of follow-up meetings in a nearby evangelical church. I went along, with my new Bible, joining nearly a hundred other young converts.

The meetings were helpful in grounding me in my new faith. I was shy, and hardly spoke to anyone, but the leaders knew what to say to us. They helped us to understand the reason for our assurance of salvation, encouraged us to read our Bibles regularly (I didn't tell them that I couldn't read at all), encouraged us to pray (which I was doing all the time), and encouraged us to enjoy regular Christian fellowship (so I began to attend the local Presbyterian church).

On my way to and from these meetings, I ran into several members of my gang. They were astonished and scornful of my conversion to Christianity. 'Two weeks, Stephen! Two weeks! That's all we'll give you! When the tent comes down your faith will disappear with it. You'll be back with us in no time!'

'No,' I said stubbornly, 'this is for keeps.' I had had the chance to have a long private talk with Shadrach Maloka, and he had prepared me for such teasing and trouble.

'The way ahead for you, Stephen, will not be easy,' he'd warned me. 'You will face persecution, from your old gang, and from other people as well. I have suffered for my faith, but Jesus will give you strength.' Then he showed me some of the scars he had received when people had literally beaten him for his faith.

In the few remaining days of the mission, I followed Shadrach everywhere. He made me very welcome. We would talk for hours, and he even let me come on his house-to-house visits. When he and the Dorothea Mission team finally had to return to South Africa, I felt I had lost my family. I felt very lonely, but determined to keep on with my new faith, and not to let Shadrach down.

Thus began a whole new way of life for me. Though of course I met with a mixed reception, I enjoyed my 'preaching' on the buses and in the market-places, so much so that for the next several weeks I spent all my days like this. I must have travelled miles on those buses, going to and from the township, witnessing to what God had done for me.

Meanwhile, I had decided to take up permanent residence under my bridge again, and searched the market until I found a bit of fairly clean sacking in which to wrap my Bible at night, to keep the sand off.

Each day on my way in and out of town I stopped to feed myself from the left-over food in the whites' dustbins. But soon there was little need for this, and I stopped, because the market traders had become friendly with me. They were generous, and gave me everything from bananas to a few shillings here and there. Then a friend, Robert, who was also drifting away from the Black Shadows, invited me round for a number of meals. He had found a job, and did not mind sharing some food with me in his little one-room house. We sat on boxes and ate gustily with our fingers. So I thanked God for each meal that I had. I wanted to eat and live. I had a purpose in life – to preach!

In between bus-rides, I'd take up a place in the market and preach from there. Soon I had a regular clientele who listened as they set out their stalls and carried on their daily business. They watched me with interest as I preached and prayed each day.

But they were growing curious over one thing, and at the end of my first week as their resident evangelist, one of them decided to mention it. 'Young man, for days you have been telling us about Jesus and how he has saved you. You preach, you pray, but you don't open your Bible. Why don't you read to us?'

I swallowed hard. 'Oh . . . that,' I said feebly. 'Next week, next week I'll read from the Bible.' My inability to read was a great embarrassment to me.

Soon after this, I ran into some more of my old comrades from the Black Shadows. After the riots they had been lying low, modestly preferring not to attract police attention. They saw me preaching in the market-place one afternoon, and walked across with total incredulity on their faces. I tentatively tried to tell them what had happened to me, but they only seized on the basic fact: 'Stephen's got religion!' as if I had caught a nasty disease.

After that, the word spread quickly among my former associates. I came in for a lot of mocking and jeering whenever they saw me. They called me 'bishop' and 'vicar', and even knelt down and pretended to cry in the street. It was embarrassing, and a bit frightening, especially when one of them pulled a knife on me. But I got away with no more than a bit of rough pushing and pulling, and hardly a scratch.

The truth was, none of my old gang cared very much what happened to me. Especially in the chaos following the riots, when many people had been arrested. Rhodesia was in such turmoil that the people in the townships had more than enough worries of their own. The fact that Stephen Lungu had 'caught religion' was the very least of my gang's problems.

Mindful of what the Dorothea Mission had told me about seeking Christian support, I joined my local

Presbyterian church in Highfield. I guess I thought that once they knew I was a new Christian, they would welcome me, and help me get started on my new life. I was penniless, homeless, unskilled, friendless (now that I had left my gang) and having to struggle for each meal. I would have been grateful for help in every and any way imaginable.

Yet when I arrived at the church and introduced myself, the welcome was all I got. Big smiles, friendly pats on the shoulder, and several 'Ah brother, bless you's, but nothing more. They did not want to know my plight, or put themselves out in any way to help me. I had given up expecting any support from my family years ago, but somehow the Christians I had met at the Dorothea Mission had made me hope that Christians were different. The Dorothea Mission had told me that local churches would help me, and so the indifference of the local Presbyterians at this time hurt me very much.

The congregation, I suppose, just did not feel comfortable with me. They were a long-established community of black folk who were very 'respectable', and to get too involved with my problems would have been a nuisance for them. So I went to church and we all smiled at each other, but inside I felt very alone and let down.

But my disappointment in Presbyterians in no way quenched my new-found faith in Jesus. He was still very real and precious to me. I still had this strong urge to tell others about the Lord. Ironically enough, even this soon got on the nerves of those good Presbyterians! My constant talk about being 'born again' and sharing this testimony in the buses and markets struck them as excessive. They thought I was some sort of fanatic.

I felt quite hurt, but kept going along on Sundays, and just kept my mouth shut when I was at church. But it was slightly embarrassing when several new faces began to appear in the church.

'Why have you come?' they'd be asked.

'We heard Stephen Lungu preaching about Jesus in the market-place and wanted to know more.'

Such additions to the congregation, as they were invariably shabby as well, did not make me popular.

Soon the elders told me that I had no right to do any public preaching unless I had their permission. I was summoned to the vestry for a scolding. The elders told me I should settle down and be a sensible Presbyterian, and just come to church on Sundays and keep my mouth shut. I replied that Jesus had saved my life, and I had to tell others about him. They said, 'Nonsense, your parents had you baptised as an infant, and that is when you became a Christian. All this talk about being born again since is nonsense.'

So I tried to co-operate, and stopped preaching for about a week. I felt terribly frustrated, and soon was back, witnessing to people in the market-place. The elders pounced, and I was put under church discipline, which meant that although I was still allowed to come to church, I was forbidden to take Holy Communion, and they cold-shouldered me on Sunday mornings.

Even so, I went along faithfully, and would continue to do so for years to come.

Meanwhile the weeks went by. I never dreamed that anyone from the Dorothea Mission would have remembered me by now. It never occurred to me that they might be looking for me. I just kept on with my simple new lifestyle – sleeping under the bridge, gleaning what I could from the markets and occasionally Robert, and preaching on the buses and in my corner of the market-place. I was so conscious of the love of God and his gracious presence during those early weeks that it never occurred to me to give up and forget about Christianity. When I prayed each day, I was given utter assurance that God was there with me.

My greatest frustration at that time was that I could not read the Bible. I had been told that it contained stories about Jesus, what he said and did. I longed so much to be able to read these. Also, my market-place congregation kept asking me to read to them, and I was running out of excuses as to why I had to say no.

One night I lay in my sandy 'grave' under the bridge, and looked at the Bible, lying in its sack beside me. I prayed wistfully, 'God, if you will open my eyes to read this Bible, I will serve you all my life.' I wasn't exactly discouraged, but I knew that I wasn't getting very far on my own. Little did I know that help was on the way.

CHAPTER TEN

THE MISSIONARY

It happened late one warm, sunny afternoon in March 1963. I was preaching in the market-place. A small crowd had gathered and I was telling once again about the night I had discovered that God was really there, when I suddenly saw a white man staring at me. He picked his way through the rotting, discarded vegetables that strewed the ground, and joined the fringe of my little audience. He listened intently, and did not take his eyes off me, but he looked at me strangely, as if he did not quite understand what I was talking about.

To my growing amazement, I realised that I knew who he was. Johannes Joubert, one of the members of the Dorothea Mission team whom I'd seen at the follow-up meetings after my conversion. My heart hammered with excitement. What was he doing here?

I stepped carefully down off the orange crate and the crowd drifted away, glancing curiously at the white man who stood there, smiling and squinting in the sunlight. In a few moments there was simply him and me there. My mouth felt all dry. I knew this man. He had been with the mission, though not at the tent on the night of the riots.

'Do you remember me?' I ventured in broken English.

He replied in Fanakalo, a mixture of English, Afrikaans and the Zulu language which is widely spoken in the mines of South Africa, and with which I was also familiar. 'You are Stephen Lungu, aren't you?' I was delighted that he remembered me. How had he found me?

'Yes,' I said.

He smiled broadly. 'I'm Hannes Joubert. I am a missionary with the Dorothea Mission.'

'I know,' I grinned. 'I remember you! You are Shadrach Maloka's friend.' Hannes Joubert was delighted that I remembered him as well, and we were soon well into explanations.

Johannes or Hannes, as he was always called, had been working with the Dorothea Mission in South Africa for a number of years. But now, following the successful mission at which I had been converted, the Dutch Reformed missionaries in Salisbury had invited the Dorothea Mission to return. The plan was for Hannes Joubert to set up a little Bible school. He had found a house in the suburb of Waterfalls.

'I am so glad to have found you, Stephen,' said Hannes Joubert. 'Shadrach told me of this special young man he had met and who had been converted during the mission. He felt a great friendship with you, and told me to look out for you. Since I have returned to Salisbury, I have been very busy working, but looking out for you as well.'

A white man looking out for me! I was deeply moved. What is this new faith I have found, I asked myself, that a white man should waste a minute's thought on someone like me? I could hardly believe it. (Although I had once hated whites deeply, I was also very much in awe of them.)

But Hannes Joubert did not allow me to become too self-conscious – he had questions for me.

'How are you doing? You were preaching this afternoon, weren't you?'

'Yes,' I admitted shyly.

'But this is wonderful! You are still strong in your faith. Who has helped you?'

'Well . . .' I thought of the disapproval of the Presbyterian church I still occasionally attended. 'No one much,' I stammered.

'What church do you go to?'

I told him, and briefly explained my problem. I had finally given up my regular attendance because they had made me so discouraged.

Hannes Joubert frowned a little. 'Stephen, you are all on your own? That is not very good.'

'But I cannot find any Christians like the ones at the tent that night.' I had a thought. 'Do *you* know of any?'

'Yes,' he said warmly, 'and they would welcome you. Would you like that?'

'Oh yes!' I said. Then I added shyly. 'I don't really know very much about Jesus. I would love to know more. I wish someone would tell me.'

Hannes Joubert paused and looked at me in a considering sort of way. 'Stephen. I have a proposition to put to you. I have told you about this Bible school I am starting. How would you like to be the very first student?'

There was such warmth and friendliness in Hannes Joubert's eyes. There was also an encouraging look that said: 'I believe in you. I believe you are up to this.' I remember the look, but I didn't see it for long, for tears sprang unbidden, and stung hot on my eyes. I brushed them away with a sleeve.

'Oh,' I breathed. This was too good to be true. A chance to learn about my new-found faith. To know people like the Christians in the tent that night. 'Oh yes, yes!' I gulped.

Hannes Joubert stretched out a thin white arm and offered me his hand. I stared at it, disbelieving, and then took it timidly. He shook my hand. His handshake was warm and firm. And very white. The handshake lasted only a moment, but I felt stunned. I blinked in the sunlight. A white man had just shaken me by the hand. I looked at my hand, back and front. I don't know what I expected – some of the white to rub off? All I knew was that I was going to Bible school and that I never wanted to wash my hand again.

Then we got down to practicalities. Hannes Joubert suggested that before I absolutely accepted, I should come and see his home at Waterfalls, a white suburb. He led the way to his combi van, and we hopped in. I revelled in the unexpected treat of a ride.

Hannes Joubert's rented home was a small, pleasant bungalow in a garden with a garage. He took me on a tour, explaining in his mix of broken English and Fanakalo that this was where he hoped to begin the classes for his Bible school, and that I was welcome to come and live with him if I would like to join – indeed, launch – the school.

I hesitated. 'But I cannot stay in your house.' Hannes Joubert nodded sad agreement: in the 1960s it was a criminal offence for a black man to live in a house in a white suburb. I would most certainly have been arrested and Hannes Joubert's Bible school would have been shut down before it opened. Hannes Joubert had already thought of a simple solution to the problem. He led me back to the garage and with a sweep of his arm asked how I would like to live here.

I looked round. It was sturdy, dry and cleaner than anywhere else I had ever lived. It had only three walls, but who was I to quibble about the lack of a fourth? Three walls were three more than I had at present under the bridge. Hannes Joubert left me for a moment, and carefully drove the combi van up to the gap and parked it sideways – thus providing the fourth wall. He jumped out of the van with a happy grin of triumph and a lump rose in my throat at his thoughtfulness.

So I nodded enthusiastically and said, 'Thank you, thank you.' Hannes Joubert said, 'You're welcome,' and we grinned some more to cover our shyness. Then he suggested, 'Why not move in today? Now!'

'Now?'

'Now! Let's get your things.'

'My things?'

'Your things.'

It was a difficult moment, and I felt very embarrassed. 'No things. No things.' I shook my head simply, then brightened up. 'Bible,' I said, holding it up. 'I have a Bible.' I smiled brightly.

Hannes Joubert paused in astonishment. 'No things? Nothing at all?' he asked incredulously.

'No.' I shook my head, ashamed. My Bible drooped at my side.

Hannes Joubert looked me over, and I was suddenly reminded of my shabbiness. Baggy, stained trousers with holes at the back, which embarrassed me terribly; soiled shirt with rips, torn slippers courtesy of a white dustbin that were tied on with bits of twine. Not much of a prospective student.

But my unglamorous appearance didn't seem to bother Hannes Joubert. His surprise was quickly overcome. He rallied quickly. 'Come on,' he said. 'You and me. Now – we are going to town.'

I raised my eyes in astonishment. He was already half-way to the van.

'Come!' he called. So I came.

There followed an hour or so of great excitement. Hannes Joubert took me shopping! It was the first time anyone had ever taken me out with the sole purpose of buying me things, and I was tongue-tied with happiness. Hannes Joubert took me downtown and bought me dark trousers, a wonderful green blazer, three white shirts, some socks, some underwear, proper shoes, two sheets, one blanket and some towels. And one steel bed complete with a mattress!

Back at the garage it took me about fifteen minutes to move me into my new home. Hannes Joubert helped me to set up my new bed in the far corner of the garage and spread my sheets and blanket over it. He produced a box into which I stashed my new trousers, socks, shirts and things. I set the Bible carefully on top, and that was it.

Then we went inside the house for a simple meal – cooked by Hannes Joubert, to my utter astonishment. A white man who rented a lovely house like this, owned a combi van, but had no black woman to cook for him. It was incredible!

Hannes Joubert's lack of a housegirl was only the first of many surprises and adjustments that faced me in my new life. But there were also shocks in store for Hannes Joubert. Like eating our first meal together that night, for example. Hannes Joubert put the food on the plates, and my mouth watered with anticipation. The smell of hot, wholesome meat and vegetables made me feel actually giddy. The plate was slipped in front of me and I was about to grab it with both hands when – 'No, Stephen, wait.' A firm hand caught my sleeve. 'First we thank God – we say grace.' Grace? Hannes Joubert closed his eyes and briefly thanked God for my safe arrival and for our supper. I could not understand all he said, but I got the general drift, and was intrigued. What a nice idea. I'd never have thought of that myself.

Then Hannes Joubert picked up his knife and fork. I eyed mine briefly. What with one thing and another in the past twenty years I'd never got as far as using a fork. There seemed little point in starting now, so I crooked my fingers and dug in. Warm vegetables were scooped up and dispatched with gusto, but the piece of meat was too big for one bite. So I propped my elbows happily each side of my plate and gnawed away, tearing hunks off with great delight. I chewed, as many Africans do, with my mouth wide open, and the food bounced off my tongue and the roof of my mouth and spun round and round like clothes tumbling in a washing machine.

Hannes Joubert shot me several glances, and I grinned widely, to show him how much his cooking was appreciated.

I bolted my food in a few minutes flat, and while I waited for Hannes Joubert to catch up with me (that fork and knife slowed him down) I ran my fingers round and round the plate and licked them to get the last drop of gravy up. I wanted to lick the plate, but I thought that might be considered rude.

Hannes Joubert looked ill at ease, for some reason. I felt concerned. Did he think I was not properly appreciative? I sat back and belched loudly and happily. He jumped. I patted my bulging stomach. He looked at it and then up at me and smiled wanly. For a few minutes we chatted in broken English/Fanakalo, but his heart wasn't really in it.

Hannes Joubert indicated that I was to help him clear the table and together we washed and dried up. I had not done this before. Under his supervision I broke only a plate and a saucer. Without him I would surely have smashed the lot.

Then Hannes Joubert indicated it was time for bed, and I

retired drowsy with excitement, and a full stomach, to the garage.

It was some time before I got to sleep, though. There were strange smells of petrol and oil, and new neighbour-hood noises to get used to. Also, I discovered that if I turned over quickly, the bed would too, and dump me on the floor. But that was a small price to pay for the happi-ness that flooded through me. God had answered my prayers more fully than I could have believed possible.

I had prayed for Christian help, and not only had I found the Dorothea Mission again, but they had given me a home. I had prayed to learn to read the Bible and I was going to be put through Bible school! I balanced carefully on my back on the bed and surveyed the future with misty optimism. All my problems were over. All that lay ahead was the joy and pleasure of learning about Jesus. That and a few other things – but who was I to know that then?

So began a whole new way of life for me. Next morning I woke stiff from my tussles with the new steel bed in the night and quickly dressed in the same old shirt and trousers I'd worn for weeks. I could not bear to use my lovely new clean ones. I decided to save them for a special occasion.

Hannes Joubert was in the kitchen. I was again amazed – a man cooking his own breakfast! That was woman's work. He looked at me as if I was a sight he did not see very often either. He paused, put down the wooden spoon he was stirring the porridge with, and beckoned me down the hallway. Timidly I followed him.

The house was so clean and neat. I was afraid I would break something. He flung open the door to his bathroom, and ran hot water into the tub. He pointed to me and then to the bath, and smiled. I smiled back, cautiously. Apart from the hospital, I had never had a bath before – all my washing had been done in rivers. Hannes Joubert indicated that I should go and get my new clothes.

What for?

To wear.

Oh dear! Obviously I had offended him by not wearing his new presents. I rushed back to the garage and got them. Back in the bathroom Hannes Joubert pointed again at me, then at the tub, and indicated the soap, and left me to it.

Gingerly I climbed into the bath. It was slippery! I hung onto the sides and lowered myself into the warm water. It quickly soaked my trousers and shirt, and felt very strange. I soaped my shirt and trousers and neck and arms and ankles and splashed about. It was difficult peeling the wet clothes off afterwards. Water was everywhere. But I felt surprisingly refreshed and invigorated. I towelled myself dry, and then wrung out my old trousers and shirt more thoroughly, slapping them noisily against the bath.

It seemed impossible to keep the water in the bath. Most of it was now on the floor of the room. I put on my new clothes, which were wet as well by this time.

Hannes Joubert's self-control when he saw his bathroom was remarkable. He gently pointed to my trousers, shirt and towel. 'Come on,' he said. He led me to a line outside. I felt strange – a man should not have to hang up washing!

But it got worse – he then led me to the kitchen and presented me with a mop. We went back down the hall to his swamped bathroom. I nearly rebelled: this was woman's work! But, well, there were no women, and I could hardly expect a white man to clean up after me. So I had a go, under his watchful eye. He smiled encouragingly while I worked, and gently explained that as a rule, clothes were washed elsewhere, and only people in bathtubs. Then I was very embarrassed.

It took quite a while to restore the bathroom. Then we went and had our breakfast to celebrate my first success-fully learned lesson at the Dorothea Mission Bible School.

The next lesson was a bit more difficult. Hannes Joubert fetched some paper, pencils and books and sat me down to discover just what level his new student was at. A little while later he got up to make some tea. He certainly need-ed it. He had just discovered that his one and only student was almost totally illiterate. Far from studying the Bible, I could barely read my own name. I could not write it. All I had was a new-found faith in Jesus, plenty of enthusiasm, several phrases of broken English, and a small working vocabulary to do with tennis balls and golf.

But missionaries are made of tough stuff. Hannes Joubert believed God wanted him to start a Bible school for black Africans in Salisbury. He had no money. He had no build-ing. He had no teachers. He had few books. He had only one student – an uncivilised twenty-year-old straight off the streets whose knowledge of Christianity came from Marxist-driven ideology, one evangelistic tent service attended with the aim of petrol bombing it, and a few fol-low-up meetings afterwards.

Many a lesser man would have caught the next train out of Salisbury. Hannes Joubert calmly prepared for the long haul. He was going to civilise me, teach me to read and write, and then he was going to put me through his Bible school. But most important of all, he was going to help my faith in God grow and mature in knowledge and experi-ence. And so we began.

CHAPTER ELEVEN

EARLY DAYS WITH HANNES JOUBERT

Sometimes at the start of a new chapter in life, it seems that everything is for you and nothing can go wrong. You feel as if you are standing on a mountain peak and can catch a glimpse of the dazzling promised land that is your future – a work to be accomplished, a relationship to be enjoyed. All is bathed in mellow, golden light.

Then as soon as you set off towards it, it seems as if the sun dips below the horizon, the vision is blacked out, and you are stumbling into a valley of problems and difficulties. You doubt you will ever be happy again.

In the days and weeks that followed my arrival at Hannes Joubert's home and the Dorothea Mission Bible School, I began to feel like that. On the face of it, everything was perfect. I had found Jesus and was assured of his love. I had been taken in by a Christian who was caring for me and teaching me the Christian faith. Compared to my old life of fear, loneliness and poverty under a bridge, it was heaven.

Only, it wasn't. Reaction had set in, for one thing, and I chaffed against the daily disciplines of an orderly existence. Nothing in my whole previous life had prepared me for it. Except for the brief rigours of the Youth League camps, my time had always been my own, with no demands on me except how to find the next meal. Now I was expected to rise at an early hour (even when I wanted to sleep more!), wash and help prepare my meals, eat with a knife and fork, wash up, do daily household chores, and then sit for a good few hours and study my English alphabet and spelling each day. The stress of it all on my undisciplined mind was intense. Hannes Joubert was kind but insistent. He pulled back only when he saw I was really desperate.

Each day began with him visiting me in the garage to make an inspection.

'Stephen, you must make your bed every morning. That means more than tugging the blanket. You must smooth it, and the sheets.

'Why is one shoe over here and the other under the bed?

'Your curtain must hang evenly – either open or shut, but not half and half.

'You must fold your clothes when you aren't in them. Don't hang shirts from the curtain rail.

'What is that plate doing under the bed?

'When your boots are muddy, take them off at the door, not after you've walked across the floor.

'Wash your clothes here.

'Wash yourself over there.

'Ironing is done before you wear a shirt. Yes – always.

'Make your bed!

'A sock should only have one hole – to let your foot in. More than that and you let your toes out again. This isn't a sock, it's a sieve. You must darn it.'

Then we would have breakfast. Wow! I hate to think of the indigestion I gave Hannes Joubert during our meals.

'Stephen, put your napkin on your lap. Open it out.

That's right.

'Stephen, your fork goes in your left hand, knife in your right.

'Eat from the fork. No Stephen, the fork, not the knife. Sit up straight. Keep your elbows down. Don't lean over your plate. You are not a vulture.

'Use your napkin for that, not your sleeve.

'Don't reach like that – ask me and I will pass things to you.

'*I saw that!*

'Stephen, when your portion of meat is that large, you don't stab the whole thing with the fork and wave it about. Cut bits off. With your knife, Stephen, NOT your teeth.'

I tried my best, honestly, but I was hungry, and the food was delicious.

'Stephen, close your mouth when you chew. Nobody wants to see what your teeth are doing to those poor vegetables.

'Stephen, say please.

'Stephen, you must chew more quietly. You sound like a pride of lions with their kill at the water hole.'

I often wondered glumly what had happened to the joy I had known and the grace of God in those early weeks as a Christian. I had thought it would just go on being like that – happy and spontaneous. I wanted to be out sharing Jesus on the buses. Hannes Joubert said I had better stay in and study my English pronunciation. Not that he was not a keen evangelist, 'but at this point in your life you have a chance to learn, and you must use it. You can be an evangelist for the rest of your life.' He hoped I would one day work with the Dorothea Mission team.

Often, to give me practice in reading aloud, Hannes Joubert would assign me to read English to Josias Ngara, another local evangelist who was blind, and who wanted to come to the Bible school. The idea was that I practise reading, and Josias transfer the book into Braille. So one morning, Hannes Joubert set us at a table outside in the garden, and told us to get on with it. We had a marvellous day, for by the end of it Josias had taught me how to tie my necktie. Being blind, he did it slowly enough for me to copy him. We were so tremendously pleased with our success that Hannes Joubert smiled and forbore to mention the lack of Braille notes and my unopened book.

As the weeks passed Hannes Joubert talked more to me, in our mix of broken English and Fanakalo, about the Dorothea Mission.

The mission had been founded in South Africa in 1942 by a white South African missionary of German descent. It was a time when the growing industrialisation of South African cities had attracted tens of thousands of blacks in search of work. Many ended poor, miserable and rootless in the burgeoning shanty towns. It was to these poor, homeless blacks that the mission was aimed.

The work grew rapidly, supported by many Christians. Then in 1962 the Dorothea Mission had felt called by God to hold a mission in Rhodesia, and had stepped out in faith. They chose Highfield and Mbare townships on the edge of Salisbury. The immediate goal was to convert a thousand people to Christ and then to launch a small Bible school. The school was to be called *Soteria* (the Greek word for 'salvation') and its function was to nurture and train some of these converts who would then form the basis of a new Dorothea Mission team based permanently in Salisbury.

When Hannes Joubert told me all this, I felt awed and overwhelmed by the graciousness of God. The night my gang and I had seen the mission, my only desire had been to destroy it. Instead, God's love had transformed me from

1964: Harare, Zimbabwe – A blind evangelist, Josias Ngara (left), writing in braille as Steve tries to read to him. Steve comments, 'I was given the task of reading to him so as to improve my reading and my English. This blind brother also taught me how to tie my necktie.'

1977: Steve's team at the Dorothea Mission.

1977: Baba and Mai Joubert.

1983: Steve's first trip to the USA.

1984: Australia – Steve comments, 'In most places my simple testimony made little children cry and respond to the gospel. These two came to talk to me and wanted to have a photo with me.'

1986: Malawi – Steve's first team in Malawi. From left, Steve, Songe and Jeremiah.

1989: Zambia – Steve preaching in the market place at the 'Lusaka Back to God' mission.

Steve's sister Malesi.

1991: Switzerland – After a week of preaching in Lausanne, the team went to the mountains so Steve could see snow for the first time. From left, Steve, Rev. Dr Edward Muhima, David Peters and Edinah Peters.

1992: South Africa – in Cape Town on the tip of Africa. Africa begins here! Steve comments, 'I remember thinking that one day I would travel across the whole continent of Africa with the gospel. Just eight years later, in 2000, I was able to preach in East, South, West and North Africa.'

1992: South Africa – Mr and Mrs Lungu.

Taking Rachel to a hotel dinner in her Ethiopian dress.

With Keith and Heide Hershey.

1994: Harare – with my mother, reunited after so many years.

1998: Pietermaritzburg, South Africa – Michael Cassidy, Founder and International Team Leader of African Enterprise, with Stephen Lungu, Team Leader, Malawi, at the AE Centre.

2000: Australia – at Ulverstone Primary School, Ulverstone, Tasmania.

an enemy into a follower of Jesus and into the very first student at the Soteria School. Such a dramatic turn around made me feel empathy with Saul on the Damascus Road, who'd also been on his way to persecute and kill Christians.

There were a few basic principles on which the mission operated. One of the most important was known as 'walking in the light' – which simply meant that we as Christians were to live in total integrity with each other. Any wrongs between us, irritations or whatever, were to be confessed and dealt with at once. 'Short accounts' were to be kept.

As long as it was Hannes Joubert and myself, this would prove easy. Though strict, he was the kindest and most straightforward of men. Later, when other students arrived, 'walking in the light' could become more difficult at times. Still, we persevered. Hannes Joubert made clear that the Soteria School put more value on how we lived our lives than on the grades we earned in his classes. You could get 100 per cent in a quiz, but still do badly in the school if you were not willing to live out the Christian ideals required. Integrity and a holy life were the most vital things of all, he told us many times.

Another concept was much harder at first: the Dorothea Mission operated 'by faith', with no salaries or long-term regular financial support. Its missionaries relied on God to provide their daily needs. In practice, this worked out through the generosity of local Christians keen to support the work. (Much of our food was provided by several Christian farmers who had made clear to Hannes Joubert that this would be part of their regular Christian stewardship.) In theory, though, living by faith held true, because Hannes Joubert's one hard-and-fast rule was that he never told his material needs to anyone but God – never to other

Christians. He had no time for 'spongers', and would never stoop to it. His deal was with God alone. For instance, you were not allowed to say to people, 'Oh, by the way, I'm trusting God for a penny stamp today.' Because then you aren't trusting God, you are begging.

So for everything – literally everything else – we depended on God alone to provide for us as he saw fit. It came as quite a shock to me. For some reason it was easier to trust God with my eternal soul than for the needs of our everyday existence.

At first I had trouble believing Hannes Joubert meant what he said: that he, personally, was penniless. For instance, we were nearly out of soap one day, so I told him we needed a new bar in the bathroom.

'I haven't got one,' he said calmly, drying the dishes.

'I'll pick one up at the market today if you'll give me the money,' I said, eager to be helpful.

He folded the tea-towel. 'Stephen, I haven't got the money for one either.' My jaw fell open in surprise.

'But . . . but . . .' I stuttered.

'You must pray and tell God about this and leave it to him,' he continued.

I went out to tidy the garden, muttering to myself. Ask God for a bar of soap? Ask God for soap? It was ridiculous. It seemed rude, even. God had more important things, surely.

Next morning the last sliver of soap collapsed and, escaping from my frantic fingers, went down the plughole. I stared forlornly after it. I wanted to go and tell Hannes Joubert about it but I knew he'd only repeat what he'd said the previous morning. For some reason, I felt quite desperate about the soap. Where were we going to get some more? So I prayed for soap. About mid-day some Christian friends of Hannes Joubert's dropped in. 'How are you,

Stephen?' They always included me in their greetings.

'Soapless,' I wanted to say, but Hannes Joubert was there, so I didn't dare. They had tea with us and went their way and we continued our study.

Late in the afternoon Hannes Joubert went out. There was a knock on the door.

Another Christian friend of ours stood there and beamed at me. 'Can't stop,' she said, 'but I went shopping this afternoon and thought some groceries might come in handy for you both.'

She thrust a brown paper bag into my hand and was gone. Trembling, I carried the bag into the kitchen. I felt that I was going to be sick with the suspense. I began pulling things out of the bag and dropping them anyhow on the floor. I ignored the many essential items this dear woman had brought us, and dug deeper and deeper. In a moment I saw them: two bars of soap, right at the bottom.

'God!' I shouted. 'You heard me!' I grabbed a bar in each hand and did a victory dance around the kitchen.

Hannes Joubert came home at that point. Once he'd realised that his student hadn't gone mad, he rejoiced with me. I learned that day that soap in itself may well be trivial, but that God can honour such reliance on him for it. It was a milestone in my early Christian life.

Another answer to prayer in those early weeks with Hannes Joubert that deeply touched me was the time I needed a postage stamp. I was writing to someone I knew who'd gone to Bulawayo, with whom I'd kept in very occasional contact. I wanted to let him know where I was now, and so I badly wanted that stamp. I dreaded having to pray for it – suppose I didn't get it? So I asked Hannes Joubert.

'Oh Stephen,' he said gently. 'You know how it is. You must not come to me for things. You must go to God. That is where I go.'

Glumly I slunk away. Here I was again, back having my faith tested. It was only for a stamp, but I found it a nerve-wracking experience. For three days I prayed for that stamp. Christian friends came and went, but never a penny. I thought I would burst with the effort of not bleating, 'Stampless!' whenever anyone asked how I was.

Then finally, just before I went completely mad, a white Christian friend dropped in out of the blue for a long chat with Hannes Joubert one evening. He was on his way out of the door when he suddenly paused. 'Oh, yes,' he said. 'I've got something for Stephen.' He thrust his hands into his pockets and produced a banknote. 'Thank you!' I gasped, and he was gone.

I sank onto the couch in Hannes Joubert's living room and stared at the money. It shook in my trembling fingers. Hannes Joubert breezed into the room. 'Stephen – are you all right? You look like you have seen a ghost.'

I held up the note. 'I only prayed for a stamp!' I whispered.

Sudden understanding swept over Hannes Joubert and he gave me a great grin. 'Well, you've enough there for a thousand stamps!'

I burst into tears. Hannes Joubert came and sat beside me.

'Stephen,' he said quietly. 'God loves you and is showing you his love through these experiences. Of course it is right that people work, and one day you may work for a wage. But at this time it is right that you are here to study and learn a new way of life, and God will provide for you. You must learn to rely on God first and fellow Christians second.'

How important this was hit home to me one day when I failed to trust God and did tell someone of my need. They graciously gave it to me, but I felt so guilty, as if I had spoiled something special between me and God. I went and confessed to Hannes Joubert and he forgave me and prayed with me.

This generosity of Christians when prompted by God would happen many times in my life, but one other very early incident happened over a pair of shoes. By now I had been with Hannes Joubert a good few months, and the cheap shoes he had bought for me (all he could afford) that first day (I now admired his step of faith in using all his money to care for me!) had finally worn out. The soles were just gone. My feet showed through the bottom. I put some cardboard in, but it moved about. I became shy about kneeling down in prayer meetings where Hannes Joubert's friends could see my feet. So in our Dorothea Mission prayer meetings I spent a lot of time manoeuvring myself into corners and making sure that when I knelt to pray, my back was up against a wall. Somehow I felt that all my past inadequacies were summed up in those shoes. They brought back vivid memories of having to tie on shoes from the whites' dustbins – of being poor, poor, poor.

In fact, those shoes so stirred up the past fears and horrors that I hadn't the faith or strength even to tell Hannes Joubert or to pray for a new pair. For in my heart I believed that I didn't really deserve decent shoes. Holey shoes were good enough for the likes of me. My self-esteem leaked out through those holes in my soles faster than the dust seeped in. Terrible fears whispered at the fringes of my mind. 'You grew up a homeless vagrant and that's all you'll ever really be.'

My misery was compounded by the fact that I had reached yet another platform in my daily struggle with learning to read and speak English. Hannes Joubert and I struggled but I was so unhappy that I felt dull and stupid.

Stupid, stupid. The daily chores and struggles with the knife and fork continued. Hannes Joubert was strict with me, and how I chaffed against it at times! Time-keeping and organisation and eating the European way just drove me crazy. (Whenever he left the table during a meal to answer the phone or door, I'd cram my food into my mouth with my hand.) I could not get the hang of it. I would fail and he would pull me up and I would feel resentful. 'Hannes Joubert is asking too much. I cannot change that much,' I would think.

'But Stephen, growing in the Christian life is all about putting off your old ways and putting on new ones. In your case, daily good manners as well as a pure life.' So I would try, and fail, and get more frustrated and want to say, 'Did St Paul use a fork?' I didn't want to be the old Stephen, but it seemed impossible to be the new Stephen. I was just Stephen, and every day was full of challenges to my old behaviour.

How Hannes Joubert stood life with me at times like this I'll never know. It was a bleak few weeks. I felt hemmed in on all sides: no relief from study, no money, no shoes. I felt so discouraged. I would never succeed. One day I sat forlornly on my steel bed in the garage and decided to leave. I packed my few things in the box that served as my wardrobe. I'd had enough. I would go and tell Hannes Joubert I couldn't stand any more and I was going.

But where? Where could I go? Back to the bridge? To fear? I felt totally frustrated. In the end I stayed, and we struggled on.

And it really was a struggle. For as well as our daily lessons for me, Hannes Joubert was trying to prepare the bungalow's grounds to become a small Bible school. He needed some more bedrooms for black people. We thought about it, and it was decided to transform the chicken coops outside into rough bedrooms. We worked hard and long at this project, cleaning, scrubbing, painting and putting in extra boards and windows. Every hour of every day was filled with work and challenges.

So we both welcomed a visiting team of workers who were on their way from South Africa to hold the first Dorothea Mission campaign in Kenya. Their merry high spirits blew a breath of wider perspective, sanity and cheer into our little house. The whispers of fear and self-hatred in my mind were stilled. These good people treated us both as valued friends. I thanked the Lord in my daily prayers for their encouragement.

One morning one of them, Thomas Barlow, drew me to one side. 'Stephen, if you aren't busy, come into town with me.' I prepared to go willingly, delighted to get out of morning study. Hannes Joubert gave me a wry knowing smile, but let me go.

Once in town, I asked Thomas where he would like me to take him. I knew he was the son of a wealthy white industrialist, and felt shy in his presence. Most young whites like him would not even have spoken to me, a poor black.

He hesitated. 'Well,' he said, 'that depends where *you* would like to go.' Then he grinned guiltily. 'You see, I want to buy you something, but I don't know what you want. So you tell me. Trousers? Shirts? Shoes?'

'Shoes?' I whispered in awe, fighting back the sudden tears. I had been unprepared for this. But Thomas took me quickly in hand and by the time we returned at lunch I was the incredulous owner of three trousers, two pairs of shoes and even a suit.

'And I only prayed for shoes!' I exulted to Hannes Joubert that evening, after the team had gone. He looked at my shining eyes and smilingly patted me on the back, but found no words to say. With my own misery lifted, a veil fell from my eyes and suddenly I saw what I should have seen months before – Hannes Joubert was desperately tired. The effort of starting a Bible school – he was receiving several interested queries now and it looked as if some more students would soon join me – and his daily watchful eye on me were beginning to tell.

Sure enough, before long, another student joined us: a Mrs Lucy Phiri. She too had never been taught how to read or write. She and Hannes Joubert had trouble understanding one another at times, and so I was brought in as the interpreter.

We worked on the verandah of the bungalow – a spacious and airy place which Hannes Joubert and I had chosen to be our Bible school's 'classroom'.

Three months after Lucy arrived, her husband followed. He was Nelson Phiri, and had worked for a sugar refinery. Then Moffat Ncube arrived. Both he and Nelson and Lucy had been converted at the same mission as me. I felt elated by their arrival – at last the Bible school was becoming a reality! Also, I so enjoyed their company. I liked people, and it was great to make new friends. Moffat and I hit it off at once. He too had come from a broken family, and had been in a gang in Bulawayo. Our similar pasts helped us to identify with each other. We both marvelled at the grace of God which had brought us to this place.

By 1964 we had all settled down to a new routine at the bungalow. The students were content in their chicken-coop bedrooms which Hannes Joubert and I had prepared so carefully for them. We students took monthly turns doing the domestic chores, including the cooking. Nobody really appreciated my attempts in the kitchen, however, and I was glad when my turn was over.

About this time another major change occurred: Hannes

Joubert found himself a wife. She was Afrikaans, and a missionary of the South African Dutch Reformed Mission serving in Rhodesia. Her name was Sustine. She moved into the bungalow with Hannes, and I now spent more time with Nelson and Moffat and the other students.

It was a good time, a time for growing together and for growing in our Christian faith. In fact, growing was the problem we had. We soon had too many students for our premises. The area, being white, would not allow so many black residents, even sleeping in chicken coops. Soteria Bible School was outgrowing her first home, and we urgently needed new premises.

CHAPTER TWELVE

DANGEROUS CRUSADES

It was 1965, and the political tension in Rhodesia was increasing all the time. Meanwhile, we members of the Dorothea Mission in Salisbury were beginning to hold regular evangelistic outreaches of our own. But though most of us were black, our preaching of what was considered to be the white person's religion was not always welcomed. One evening it landed us in extreme danger.

We were to hold a tent meeting in Harare (now Mbare) township. That afternoon we set off in pairs as usual to distribute tracts and handbills around the neighbourhood, letting people know about the meeting. As usual, we were due to meet up back at the tent shortly after five. We had lights to put up, the PA system to sort out, supper to eat, and music to arrange.

I was with Josias, the blind member of our team, and we had had a discouraging afternoon. People had been quite surly with us, and reluctant to accept our handbills. They said sharp things to us as well, such as 'this is white junk' or 'you are sell-outs' or 'you are the white man's servants'. Still, we carried on as best we could.

As five o'clock approached, Josias and I were heading

back for the tent. By now the roads were crowded with people going home, on foot and by bicycle. Suddenly I noticed a trail of little bits of paper all along the ground. That paper looked familiar to me. I stooped for a closer look, and my suspicions were confirmed. They *were* our handbills! There must be other members of our team a little way in front of us, handing them out, and people were tearing them up at once. It was not an encouraging sight, and I told Josias about it as we followed that ominous little trail of ripped shreds all the way back to our tent.

The other members of our team had had similar troubles that afternoon, and we discussed it over supper by the tent. We decided that the people leaving work in the area must be very tense, with all the local political problems. However, there were many thousands of people in Harare, and we hoped that we had distributed enough handbills so that those who *did* want to hear the gospel would come to our meeting that night.

So we rigged up our PA system, put up the lights, and prepared for the service. As 7 pm approached, and people began to arrive, I played the accordion and Moffat Ncube took his place at the front to act as music director.

There was an immediate problem. People were coming, yes, and listening, yes, but they would not enter the tent, and there were no women or children among them. This was uncanny, unheard of. Where had all the women and children gone? Also, the men who were arriving would not sing along to our choruses. Again and again Moffat invited them to join in the cheerful tunes that I was playing. But they would not. Indeed, they kept refusing to even enter the tent, except for a handful of young men who came inside and sat uneasily on the benches. The rest stood obstinately outside, silent. It was uncanny. As the minutes slid by, some members of our team went out to see what was going on. They were amazed to find that a very large crowd of men indeed had gathered, and more were still arriving. Whatever was going on? It was becoming very intimidating.

Suddenly there was the most unearthly shriek, a blood-curdling cry, and out of the darkness a man in a frenzy rushed in upon us. He had spotted the two white members of our team, Harold and Evert, sitting near the front. He rushed up to Harold, waving his arms, his face deranged with fury. We were all so shocked, that none of us reacted at all. This was probably the best thing we could have done, for after a few minutes the man turned and sloped out of the tent again, still making strange cries.

But the crowd of hundreds of men still stood outside our tent. They were ominous in their silence and their stillness. They simply stared at us. No one so much as waved a threatening arm. Instead, they kept their hands well behind their backs. (We found out why a few minutes later.)

Meanwhile, another young man had slipped quickly into the tent. He had not come to attack us, but to warn us. He did not mince his words. He said simply: 'Hey guys, if you want life, you must leave.' With that, he vanished, slipping back into the night. (We met that young man again, in happier times. He became a Christian, and eventually joined the Dorothea Mission as an evangelist.)

Meanwhile, our team looked at each other. 'Guys, we must leave,' said one of us. No one disagreed. Several made immediately for the van, while the rest of us quickly gathered our equipment. I packed my accordion and carried it out to the van. In front of me were dozens of silent, watchful men. It was unnerving to have to walk out from the tent and face such hostility. Several members of the team scrambled into the back of the van and sat on the benches. I noticed that no one had brought Josias, our blind team member, and so I hurried back to get him. At this moment, harsh singing began: 'The freedom you are crying for has come . . . with Nkomo!' It was a popular political rallying song, and carried much hatred of anything white with it. I knew it well – I had sung it myself many times in the days before my conversion.

My friends in the van sat nervously listening to this singing all around them, while I led Josias out to the van. Then I remembered that I had left one of our lamps in the tent. They were expensive, and so I rushed back to collect it as well. I dumped it in the back of the van, swung the doors shut, and quickly made my way alongside the van towards the front passenger seat. My route took me in front of the crowd, whose singing was rising in volume and intensity, their anger growing. I jumped into the van, shut the door, and caught a glimpse of all those angry faces. I felt very vulnerable with only a sheet of glass between us. The sides of our van were metal, and I decided I'd be safer in the back, with more than a thin sheet of glass to protect me. I turned and was about to dive over the front seat into the back, when Harold started the engine.

The sound of the engine did it. The crowd went mad. A hailstorm of rocks and bricks flew through the air, smashing against the side of the van. (Now we realised why they had held their hands so carefully behind their backs!) At that instant a huge brick smashed through the passenger window. Only the fact that I had turned and was leaning into the back of the van saved me from serious injury. The brick would have smashed right into the side of my head. As it was, it just brushed my back. But it was travelling with such force that it crashed into Harold's left knee, the one he needed to push the clutch. He screamed in agony.

'Drive, *Drive*!' I shouted.

'I can't!' he cried. 'My knee!'

'Drive, brother! Get us out of here!'

He struggled frantically, trying to get his smashed knee to operate the clutch.

Then somebody in the back of the van shouted: 'Where is Zwane?'

As rocks continued to rain down upon us with a deafening roar, we all looked at each other in horror. Zwane was a South African member of the Dorothea Mission, who had come to help our team. Where on earth was he in all this chaos?

'Drive!' I shouted to Harold again.

'I can't leave Zwane!' he shouted back.

'We cannot help him now!' The rain of stones against the van was quite deafening. Other windows were cracking all around us.

Harold understood the hopelessness of our trying to rescue Zwane when our own lives were in such a precarious position. He finally managed to slip the clutch, and off we went, leaping along like a frightened kangaroo. We picked up speed, and thundered past the threatening crowd, heading for the main road.

'Where are we going?' shouted Harold, trying to control the racing van, and nursing his shattered knee

'The police station! The police station! Go there!' I shouted. It was two kilometres away, and I knew if we could reach it we would be safe.

We were fortunate, and did make it to safety. The policemen were sorry to hear of our attack, but not in the least surprised. But – where was Zwane? We told the police about him, and persuaded them to go and look for him. 'He will not know what to do,' we explained to the police. 'He is a stranger here.'

The police used the loudspeaker on one their landrovers, and slowly trawled the area, calling his name. After an hour or so, to our immense relief, Zwane appeared out of the night, and the police landrover brought him in safely. He told us that he had panicked at the sight of the crowd, and instead of joining us in the van, had decided he'd be safer slipping under the tent itself and pretending to join the crowd. No one had bothered with him, but he had been lost and very frightened in the angry crowd. (We heard next day that the hessian base around the sides of tent and the benches had been set on fire and several people in the township injured.)

We finally got back to the mission headquarters in Westwood by about 11 pm. We were exhausted but philosophical over our near escape from death. Evangelism in Rhodesia in those days carried risks, but we had already counted the possible cost, and were willing to risk death for the joy of winning souls. No one was sleepy, and so instead we sat and planned the next day's work, which was more evangelism, but this time to the many workers on one of the local farms.

Next morning we set off. My going with them accidentally precipitated a family crisis. For my cousins in Highfield, who knew I'd been preaching, had heard of the attack on the tent in Harare, and were told that I had died. My aunts, who had shown little or no interest in my life, were very eager to mourn my death. They decided to give me a huge funeral.

They began the preparations while the cousins were sent to collect my body. There entailed a great fuss when my body could not be found. There were accusations that Dorothea Mission would not admit that I had been killed. Soon a telephone message from a sorely exasperated Dorothea missioner to the farm brought me back to

Westwood to prove that news of my death had been exaggerated. My aunts retired with ill grace, grumbling that I had always been unreliable.

In the months following the Harare township riot, more missions were planned. The policy of the Dorothea Mission in those days was to send up one of their white staff to lead our missions in Salisbury. Because I could understand English well by this time, and of course spoke Shona fluently, I became their interpreter.

I was delighted to interpret for my white South African colleagues, and as the months rolled by I found myself increasingly getting out on missions and away from Bible school study. This suited me fine, except that the more conscientious teachers (there were several by now) would give me some lessons to take along and study.

Their efforts with me were a case of the triumph of hope over experience, because once I was on the trail, I never found time to study. My heart went out to the people to whom we had gone to minister, and I spent all my time with them instead. This helped me learn about ministry, but did not help me get good marks in my exams!

The Dorothea Mission teachers gradually accepted this, and during 1965 I moved quietly over onto the full-time team, also based at the Soteria School in Westwood. It was obvious that the scholastic world wasn't going to make a great deal of me. I was a people person.

Thus I became a full-time evangelist at a time when Africa was being rocked by political turmoil and change. I might not have had the best of educations, a deep understanding of theology or a vast vocabulary, but I had one great advantage: I had lived the harsh, lonely life of the people we were trying to reach. I knew what Jesus had done for me and could do for them. I was eager to tell everyone what I had found. I knew I was called by God to be an evangelist, and for that one role my whole life had superbly equipped me. It was a case of the disciple saying, 'Come and see,' or the blind man in the New Testament saying, 'All I know is that I was blind and now I see.' That summed up my ministry perfectly, and that is how I wanted to spend the rest of my life.

Another highlight of 1965 was the occasional chance to meet up with Shadrach Maloka, the South African Dorothea missioner whose preaching had first drawn me down the aisle of the tent meeting. We became great friends, and worked well together. He would preach and I would testify – I was living proof of his words. As the Americans say, that would really 'sock it to them'.

I loved Shadrach Maloka – the night of the riot had formed a bond between us; I owed my life and soul to him. Many times I would sit down with him and ask him all the things that puzzled me. I never felt overawed by Shadrach. He had also been rejected by his parents, and had had to survive on his own. This encouraged me greatly. I reasoned: if God can do these things with this man, surely he can do the same with me?

Shadrach was so loving and gracious. He would answer all my questions and pass on the lessons he'd learned in how to be most effective in ministering for God. I admired his total seriousness, and how he made time for people.

We also shared the dangerous, precarious life of evangelism in Africa in the mid-1960s. One such incident was on a mission to Zambia. At a large open-air market in Ndola, Shadrach started to preach. My sensitive political antennae warned me that this was not a good time or place to preach – there had been a political demonstration that very day. I sensed the emotional turbulence among the people, the barely controlled anger.

Shadrach did not understand my fears, and dismissed

them: 'We must be men.' But if the mob went for us, what sort of men would we be in a little while from now? So I helped with singing and then stood near Shadrach as he began to preach. I had two completely untypical feelings for me: stage-fright, and the hope that no one would take the slightest notice of Shadrach.

But of course his voice carried, and he attracted the attention of the mob. I learned that day how a red rag feels when it flutters before a bull. Angry men soon stormed over and tore our Bibles in pieces in front of us. They demolished our simple microphones and amplifier. They grabbed Shadrach and threw him back and forth between them like a rag doll. They tore his jacket and beat him. I tried to stop them and they beat me, slapping my face and jeering. They stoned the car and humiliated the two white missionaries with us.

My anger at what they were doing to Shadrach overcame my fear and I struggled in their arms, suddenly furious and desperate to fight back. But at the same instant came a clear inner voice urging me instead to kneel and pray. I was helped to the ground anyway, because at that point someone knocked me over. So I stayed down and prayed. This caught their attention, and they jeered at me, leaving Shadrach alone. Police came a few minutes later, and the crowd surged on, leaving all of us at least still alive.

Shadrach apologised afterwards for not heeding me. But I had also learned something. I felt God reminding me that preaching would take me into the violent world in which I had found my own faith. If I was to succeed as an evangelist, it was vital to have counted the cost now, and to put my life in God's hands.

This need to be prepared for anything and to hold our lives lightly was brought home soon afterwards in a different mission, this time in Malawi. Our team was preaching in a small village right by Blantyre Chileka Airport, and up to three thousand people had come to hear us from villages round about. Otto Kapia, a member of the South African Dorothea Mission team, preached and then invited me to share my testimony.

Many came forward, weeping at Otto's call, and we did not get back to the local elder's house until midnight.

I went to bed on top of the world. What a success our meeting had been! People had told me that a local political rally had been all but empty as people had come to us instead. My insecurities meant that any success went to my head far too easily in those days. I lay in the darkness grinning to myself. 'We've done it!' We certainly had.

Soon Otto, the Malawi pastor who was our host, and I fell fast asleep, tired out. But at 1 am there was a commotion at the door. I dragged myself out of bed. 'Can't they wait until morning to come to us for counselling?' I asked myself sleepily. I opened the door and woke up fast. This was no group of repentant Christians. This was a small band of very angry local members of the Malawi Congress Party Youth League. They were notorious for their violence and harshness towards anyone who opposed the Government. They seized me, Otto and the Malawi pastor.

'You are bringing discord and chaos to this place!' they hissed. 'Come with us!' We were dragged into the bush. They did not understand in the least what was happening at our meetings, but they were very irritated at having had their own meeting boycotted in favour of us. So they tied our hands behind our backs and walked us several miles into the bush, threatening to tie us in sacks and hurl us into the nearby Shire river.

As I was hustled along, I battled with my fear. Then my wits began to come back to me. 'Ah well, Jesus suffered for me, and now I am going to suffer for him.' That reminded me of how my namesake Stephen in the Bible had suffered and been martyred.

I took sudden comfort in this, and felt just a scrap of courage return to me. I was going to die. All right, I would die a Christian death. Otto suddenly began singing one of my favourite choruses, 'There is power, power, wonder-working power.' The pastor and I joined in.

The men told us to be quiet.

'Well,' I gasped politely, 'we are singing to God because we are going to die for him.'

No one disagreed with this.

Soon we reached thick bush and the hide-out of the leader. He woke up quickly and cast a lantern over us and his men in stern astonishment.

'Why bring these men here? What crime have they committed against the Party?' For these men, the Malawi Congress Party was everything.

'They were preaching the night of our rally.'

The leader rolled his eyes in exasperation. 'Do you want to fight with God and punish his men for preaching? Do you want to alienate all the people against us? Untie these men.'

Then he roughly ordered the leaders of our kidnappers to be tied and whipped.

Otto and I objected. 'Please don't touch them. We would like to invite them all to come to our meetings instead.'

The leader shrugged his shoulders, and said to us, 'Be gone.' It was obviously none of our business how he punished his men.

So we started walking back through the bush. We finally got back to our village at dawn. To our amazement, we found that hundreds of people had spent the night praying for us. The news of our kidnap had leaked out and alarmed the village. Now our safe return aroused great rejoicing. Later that day even more people turned out for our meeting. Many were touched and decided to become Christians. We went home to Salisbury utterly exhausted but very happy.

Of course, not every mission was a brush with death. We would often sleep in our truck, and do our daily preaching in market-places, and although people would pause to listen, very few would respond. I sometimes found this very depressing, but Shadrach was brisk with me. 'Don't take it personally. We are being faithful witnesses, and God will use us to prepare people as well as to bring them to conversion now.'

God also used us to bring people to conviction about past sins. Another time Shadrach, Nelson and I were ministering in Malawi. I had shared my testimony, and mentioned that the day after my conversion, I had given myself up to the police because I wanted to put things right in my life. That night we went to bed, and someone began pounding on the door at 2 am in the morning. Sleepily, I answered the door.

It was an elder of the church, wrapped in a blanket, in floods of tears. He said that God had convicted him, and that was all we could get out of him for some time. Finally he told us what was bothering him.

'Fifteen years ago, when we built the church, I was given money to buy the roof and timber and tiles for the building. But I kept the money, and stole or bribed to get the materials for the church.' We prayed with him as he tried to decide how to put things right.

Next day he went off to the local factory and confessed that he had stolen the goods. He explained that he wanted to make restitution, and if they wanted to arrest him, well and good. The factory manager, as soon as he could speak, said, 'If God has forgiven you and you have been brave enough to confess, tell me when you build another church and I will give you some things for it free to thank God.'

That evening the elder burst into our meeting jumping for joy. When he'd told his story there was no need for preaching that night. Many people were converted.

Back at Soteria Bible School in the mid-1960s, Hannes Joubert called us all together. He had some momentous news: the Dorothea Mission in South Africa had decided the time had come to set up a proper team in Salisbury. They were sending Patrick Johnstone, a young Englishman in his twenties, to Salisbury to set it up and lead it, while Hannes Joubert continued to train new Christians at the Soteria Bible School.

I was greatly excited. I had met Patrick on one of Dorothea Mission's annual prayer conferences in South Africa, when all the teams got together. I liked Patrick right from the start. As with the other English people I had met, I found that he treated all of us blacks well, and with no sign of apartheid. It made for warm and friendly relations. (However, it got him into some trouble with the Afrikaans team members of the Dorothea Mission. For all their sincere Christian faith, these dear people still maintained a very paternalistic attitude towards us blacks. We were kept at a distance, and always made to do any manual work required, never the whites. In doing this, of course, our South African colleagues were only obeying the law of South Africa at the time. But sadly, it made for a 'them' and 'us' sort of set-up within the mission.)

Patrick Johnstone arrived at Soteria, and settled in amid warm welcomes. His first priority was to get to know the 'graduates' of our Bible school which would make up his team. There were eight of us, including my closest friends, Josias Ngara, and Moffatt Ncube. Nelson Phiri did not join our team at this time, as he was appointed house-father to the school, and made an excellent job of it.

After all my trials and tribulations with Hannes Joubert, I suppose I was expecting clear sailing with Patrick Johnstone. After all, by now I could use a knife and fork, always made my bed, and ironed my shirts. I could also write and speak simple English. What more could anyone ask of me? I felt so civilised that at times I could hardly believe it was still me.

It didn't take me long to discover that I had climbed out of the frying pan and fallen straight into the fire.

CHAPTER THIRTEEN

PATRICK JOHNSTONE

Patrick Johnstone was a highly intelligent, methodical, rigorous perfectionist who in his enthusiasm for the gospel was determined to help us, his fellow evangelists, become the best we could be. He spent his first six months with us getting to know us individually. He got acquainted with each one of our weaknesses, strengths and special gifts. Patrick had a profound love for the Bible, and made it his aim to help us dig deep

Patrick Johnstone's aim was clear: he believed that we each had had a calling from God to be evangelists, and he was determined to make us as effective as possible. Unlike many white missionaries of that era, he was not one for maintaining white supremacy. He saw clearly the desperate need for training black African Christians for leadership in the African church.

I, for one, knew what I badly wanted to become, and I welcomed Patrick Johnstone's help. But when we started I had no idea of the personal cost in tears and sheer effort. I supposed that culture and learning were a veneer that would be slapped on top of me. Little did I guess that in acquiring it, I would necessarily be taken apart and put back together properly.

Our conflicts did not begin all at once, for Patrick was busy making Christian contacts throughout Salisbury and in planning how to launch his team in the most effective manner possible. In doing so he introduced the routine used by the Dorothea Mission in South Africa. It would become our way of life for the next thirteen years.

The Dorothea Mission's first priority was that our lives should be built around prayer, study and outreach. They also believed that for an outreach to be really effective, a mission should run for about a month in one place. Thus our days were quickly filled. Mornings were devoted to prayer and preparation, while each afternoon we began spending three hours out and about, visiting Christians to prepare for meetings, or visiting house to house. We would encourage converts in their new faith. By late afternoon, about 4.30 pm, we would hold a simple open-air meeting to catch people's attention on their way home from work. By seven we were down at the tent, preparing for the evening's rally.

In such a way, from about 1966 until the late 1970s, we would manage to hold a campaign in almost every town in Rhodesia, as well as in towns in Mozambique, Malawi, Zambia, Botswana and South Africa.

Within a year of his arrival, the Dorothea Mission in South Africa changed its mind about having Patrick develop a team in the same place as the Soteria Bible School in Westwood, Salisbury. They decided to transfer Patrick several hundred kilometres south to Bulawayo, where he would base a team in Matebeleland. This would have two advantages: it would give the Dorothea Mission yet another base in Rhodesia, and would also allow Patrick to develop his particular dream, which was training us for black leadership.

In this, Patrick was remarkably far-sighted. He could see the future of Africa, and knew that white dominance would become obsolete. He wanted therefore to prepare us black evangelists for leadership. He wanted so much more than just to lead a team of eight black Africans: he wanted to prepare us to lead our own teams in due course. In the meantime, this would involve continually stretching us to our limits – and sometimes to our breaking points.

Especially me. For it wasn't very long after Patrick arrived at Westwood that he seemed to be focusing in on me as his special prodigy. Many an evening he would invite me over to his small caravan in the grounds of the Bible school for a meal and a good chat. I was delighted and encouraged by this, except that it was also uncomfortable at times.

For instance, Patrick soon decided that I should be taken out and about with him. He wanted to introduce me as an equal wherever we went, including to visit his white friends. He loved me as a colleague, and wanted me to be myself in front of his friends.

Well! This was a new idea even to the Dorothea Mission. And here Patrick had touched the inner core of all that the years had made me. All my insecurity, and my conviction that I was a total nobody, came back to unnerve me. It made me terribly shy.

'I can't go to a white man's house!'

'Yes, you can.'

'But what will I say to him? He won't want me.'

'Yes he will.'

Patrick had it out with me as to the theory many times: God created you, he died for you – you are as good as anyone. You have had less chances: that is not your fault.

Practice was another. In the course of our work together, we'd often visit the homes of various white Christian friends. At first I'd shuffle in behind him, eyes meekly downcast. Patrick would introduce me. 'Good day, sir,' I'd start to say.

Patrick would glare. 'Ssss' I'd fizz, and slowly I'd force my head up and look the man timidly in the eye. We'd be invited to sit down. I'd sit small in a corner, limbs wrapped up tight, eyes down. The host would leave for refreshments and Patrick would readjust my posture.

'Don't shuffle! Sit back! Relax! Sit big! Get those shoulders back! Head up! Relax! Don't wind your legs around each other. Stretch them out in front. Relax! Smile!'

Relax? The host would return to find me bolt upright, shoulders stiff, chest out, legs out, with a glazed look on my face and a fine show of teeth. I looked rather as if I'd been stabbed in the back and rigor mortis was now setting in.

Finally, we'd leave. Patrick caught me bowing one time early on and nearly did me an injury with the silent thump he gave me. As I limped away home with him, he was adamant: 'No Stephen. He is not the Queen of England – he is a man like you or me.'

Like you or me. Patrick was a man in a million. He was a true gentleman. Light years above me in learning, he was determined to pull me up to his level. He might have wanted to murder me many times, but it was out of frustration, never contempt.

He even, sadly, had to disagree with some white Christian missionaries from South Africa over this stand of his. They were shocked when on a visit they learned that I called Patrick by his first name. They took me to one side and explained my 'error', abashing me completely in the process.

Later that day I came upon them all having tea together, and I needed to tell Patrick something. 'Mr Johnstone,' I said timidly, to attract his attention.

Nothing. Patrick took a sip of tea and began to talk to someone else. 'Mr Johnstone,' I repeated, with a quaver.

Nothing. The missionaries looked at me as if to say, 'Why are you disturbing him now?' I felt sick with embarrassment.

Patrick had never ignored me before. Obviously they had got hold of him and reminded him of my social place. I felt tears prick my eyes. If my message had not been urgent, I would have fled there and then. But I just had to let him know. 'Patrick,' I said desperately, and then gasped – I'd really done it now!

'Steve?' Immediately Patrick swung round on me with a welcoming smile on his face, giving me his full attention. He positively beamed at me.

A lump came into my throat as understanding flashed upon me. I loved Patrick that day. He was given me by God to help me. The missionaries looked scandalised and withdrew in a collective huff. Long afterwards I learned that they had warned Patrick that it was dangerous to let me call him by his first name.

Patrick had said mildly: 'We call him Stephen, why not vice versa?'

'It will lead to communism.'

Next day Patrick had to go out, and the missionaries descended on me again. They told me that it was my duty to wash their cars and sweep for them while they stayed. They said they hoped very much that I would learn humility by always doing all the cars and all the sweeping.

I felt hurt by their obvious contempt. I had always happily swept and washed for Hannes Joubert – I loved him and revered him as a father. The subject had simply never arisen with Patrick – we had taken it in turns. Within the hour, sure enough, Patrick roared up in a muddy van. The missionaries gathered in a pack on the porch and gave me meaningful, tight-lipped stares.

Oh dear, I thought, here we go. Unwilling to let Patrick down, I went and filled a bucket and advanced on his van. Timidly I offered to wash it.

Patrick glanced swiftly up at the missionaries. 'Nonsense,' he said loudly. 'I made it dirty. I'll wash it, Stephen. Why on earth should you?'

The missionaries left next day. 'You are dabbling with Marxism,' was their verdict.

I can't honestly say I was sorry to see them go.

The months flew by. Even when Patrick moved to Bulawayo, I saw him often, spending weeks at his spacious new home in Matabeleland. Patrick continued to winch me slowly up to ever-increasing levels of social, mental, emotional and spiritual maturity. I crawled along, leaning heavily on his help. From each plateau of increased understanding and better behaviour I would look back down, dizzy with the heights I had already reached.

But Patrick would never let me rest. He was forever urging me on. How he worked me! My English was good by now, but even so, Patrick was determined that I should learn to speak and read fluent English. He even threw in a little arithmetic for good measure because he decided I should be able to do simple accounts.

'Stephen – read the newspapers, the Bible, these books. Yes, read!'

'No, that's poor English. You say . . . .'

'Yes, those letters together may look like they sound like that but they are pronounced . . . .'

'Stephen, your pronunciation there is poor. Stephen, don't slur.'

It was work, work, work. This got me down at times, but Patrick persevered. He had the wider vision of what the clay could become one day. As the unhappy lump on the potter's wheel, I was only conscious of the pain of being pulled out of the only shape I'd ever known, and stretched and pinched in new, uncomfortable ways.

Sometimes the clay rebelled. Especially with regard to time-keeping. After all, I was an African. In Africa, if you are one hour late, you are right on time. In Patrick's book, if you were one minute late, you were LATE. When I showed up an hour or two after an agreed time, he was beside himself. Curious how a white person could go so red.

'Stephen, nine o'clock means nine o'clock. It does not mean eleven o'clock.'

He'd reproach me for time-keeping in front of the other evangelists, which I found embarrassing.

One day I nearly killed myself to be on time for him. 'Stephen,' he snapped as I arrived. 'You are ten minutes late. When will you learn?' When four other evangelists arrived half an hour later still, with little comment from Patrick, that did it.

I went back to my room seething with resentment. I hated Patrick and was convinced that he must hate me too. I did not stop to think that I was his special prodigy. I saw myself only as his special victim. 'He always scolds me.' He had it in for me. I'd had enough.

I packed my box and stalked out of the house. I would go and live back in Salisbury.

Patrick caught up with me half way down the street and all but dragged me back. 'Where do you think you are going? After all the effort I've put into you, do you think I'll let you go now? Your place is with us, and it's time you tried harder. You are going to become the best you can be, or I'll kill us both in the process.' I did not doubt it.

But the daily frictions went on, and it usually seemed as

if I could do nothing right. Moan, moan, moan. It did not help that our personalities were diametrically opposed. I was a person of emotions: if I felt, I acted. My head didn't often get in the way. Patrick was a man of careful thought. Emotional swamps were anathema to him. So we were on each other's nerves constantly.

'Such a harsh man,' I'd tell my pillow at night.

Finally, thank God, that rainy season had ended and the season of mission began. Through 1966, and then 1967 and 1968 we held back-to-back missions for nine months of every year.

The pattern for planning, staging and winding up a mission was very much the same wherever we went. Having secured an official invitation from a church or churches to hold a mission in their area, Patrick would first arrange where the meetings would be held. Sometimes it was the church itself, other times the large tent owned by the Dorothea Mission.

But that was just the beginning of the work involved. Patrick then went about informing the police, getting their permission, sorting out tents and chairs, informing all the local churches, organising music, organising teams of counsellors, planning the services. Under Patrick, everything went like clockwork. I would watch with mounting glee, eager for the night itself. Patrick would smile at my enthusiasm, but try and get my attention on the details of preparation ahead of time.

Once the mission was underway, we would stay in that place for anything from three to five weeks, preaching each evening, and counselling new converts each day. Time and again we met the problems of witchcraft, drugs, drink, and the need for new Christians to set their lives in order. We always encouraged new converts to link up with their local churches, who would then support them when we left.

As the years went by we travelled the rutted African roads from Rhodesia to Malawi, from Bulawayo to Botswana and Zambia, and even to South Africa. We prayed, we studied, we visited thousands of homes, we spoke in hundreds of market-places and anywhere else we had the chance. The team worked together, prayed together, argued together, and shared times of deep friendship. Patrick applauded my talent for the piano-accordion and told me I was 'a natural' at it. It gave me such great delight to find something of worth in myself. As we travelled and worked and shared our lives so closely, we were gradually being forged into a strong and effective evangelistic unit. Meanwhile, we constantly stayed in places and ate food that made me glad that my childhood had prepared me to eat anything and sleep anywhere. Patrick liked sweet tea, and we used to tease him by adding even a few more spoonfuls when he wasn't looking. Of such teasing friendships are made.

For every week away, we got a day off, and much of this was spent simply recovering from our exhaustion. We were all poor, with never more than our basic needs met. But in happiness and contentment we were rich and satisfied. My only desire in life was to share my faith with anyone who would listen. Jesus had given me life and I craved to share this good news with everyone.

And slowly, as the years went by, I did indeed change my behaviour patterns. My shyness gradually left me. The awkward new ways of speaking and acting became familiar, then comfortable, until finally, imperceptibly, they themselves became habitual. Naturally, all my new attitudes and values were modelled solely on Patrick Johnstone. The other students teased me: 'You are just like Patrick – you hate lateness and you want everything just so.' I was astonished. He was so rigorous and meticulous in all he did, how could I ever reach that standard?

By the late 1960s I had dozens of Christian friends in several different countries, and dozens of opportunities for evangelism. Patrick and I were on the best of terms, and I was happy and completely satisfied with life – or so I told myself. But there was one thing missing, and as a normal young man in my late twenties, I found it hard to ignore: I was lonely for a wife.

My loneliness and yearning grew when Patrick announced that he himself was to marry an English Dorothea missionary working in child evangelism in South Africa. She was called Jill. In Africa a young man leading a celibate life is unheard of, and I certainly found it difficult at times. But the problems surrounding me getting married seemed insurmountable. Apart from the fact that I did not want to marry any of the many young women I knew, I was personally penniless. So even if I found a young woman whom I wanted to marry, why would she want to marry me? I had a job, certainly, but no salary, and no house and no furniture. I could still get all my worldly possessions into a suitcase.

Also, worst of all, was my deep personal fear of failure if I did get married. What kind of husband would I be? I would want to be the best sort of husband, but I feared that I might let my wife down. The tragedy of my parents' marriage haunted me, and I was terrified that I would become like my father. So for seven years now I had prayed and thought about marriage, but had done nothing. 'God,' I prayed, 'if you want me to marry, please prepare me and take out anything in my life that might spoil my future wife's happiness.'

One day, while I was praying, I had a sort of waking vision. It was strange. In my vision I saw a young woman seated before me, dressed in a loose blue outfit of some kind. She was holding a Bible, but it was upside down. Nevertheless, in my vision I could still see what page it was opened at – Acts 26. This was highly significant to me, because the Lord had used Acts 26:15–19 in my own life. Nothing happened after this vision, yet it came again to me most clearly two more times over the following two years. I thought about it occasionally, and wondered what it could mean.

CHAPTER FOURTEEN

RACHEL

'Why don't you learn to drive?' Patrick suggested one day. I was appalled. 'What if I crashed that expensive van? Hannes Joubert had started to teach me some while before, but pressure of time had stopped him, and so he now suggested that Patrick teach me.

Our first lesson was a disaster. Patrick was impatient with my mistakes. 'Stop grinding the gears, and slow down! You are not being chased by rioters now!' My way of hiding my timidity was to take a running jump at things.

Several lessons later, Patrick had taught me to drive. For practice, he'd let me drive from the Bible school in Westwood, through all of Salisbury and out to our current mission at St Mary's, Chitungwiza. The traffic was a nightmare, but Patrick encouraged me, and then astonished me by declaring I was a 'natural' at the wheel. In December 1967 my ability to drive would change the course of my life.

It happened this way. A friend in Salisbury needed to get to Malawi just before Christmas to install his two daughters in a Christian boarding school there. He asked me if I would drive them, because he had no licence. I tentatively approached Patrick to ask him. We were still three days away from the close of a mission, and Patrick usually insisted on all evangelists staying until a mission was over. This time, however, Patrick agreed to let me go.

I drove the eight hours to Lilongwe and we dropped off the girls, as planned. Then on our way back to Salisbury, we stopped off at Blantyre to visit a Christian family we knew. The wife had been at Soteria Bible School with us. As it was so close to Christmas, the family kindly asked us to stay overnight, and we agreed. That first evening, as we talked about the Dorothea Mission outreaches, the family began telling us of this terrific young girl they knew who worked at Barclays Bank.

'She should be with the Dorothea Mission too. She testifies and preaches in her lunch-break on the street!'

Kennedy, the son of the family, who had been converted during one of our missions to Malawi with Shadrach, had heard my story and turned to me now. 'That's just like you,' he grinned mischievously. 'You should meet Rachel.'

I laughed. 'Sure,' I said.

A few days later, Kennedy invited me to be guest speaker at a local youth-group meeting at the Good News Bookroom in Blantyre. After I preached, people came forward for counselling, while others started to leave. Something made me pause to talk to one of the young men leaving, and ask him about his certainty of salvation. He seemed confused, but interested. He told me his name was John, and invited me to his home to talk further, when he had more time. As I was speaking to him, my eye was caught by the person seated just beyond him. It was a girl in a loose blue outfit, holding a Bible upside down. The page was open at Acts 26. I could not believe my eyes, and after staring, turned hastily away. My heart was hammering, and I felt very confused. What was this about?!

The following day was Christmas. After church in the morning, I decided to visit John, the interested young man of the day before.

I followed his instructions, and found the house easily. But the houseboy told me John had just gone out. Seeing my disappointment, he invited me in anyway, and then told me to wait a moment. Then a young woman appeared. I could not believe my eyes. It was the lady in my vision again. An electric current of excitement tingled all over me.

She gave me a warm, welcoming smile. 'I am so sorry that my brother has let you down,' she said. 'But do come in.'

Shyly I introduced myself. 'I'm Stephen Lungu, from the Dorothea Mission.'

'I know,' she said. 'I heard you speaking yesterday. And I'm Rachel,' she smiled. 'I was so glad you were speaking to my brother yesterday. I was praying that he would listen.'

I stood there wondering how to tell her that I had been having visions about her for two years. All I could find to say was: 'I've heard of you from the Mkumba family. Tell John I was here, and hope to see him again soon.' A few minutes later I staggered out of the house on cloud nine. I was so excited that I did not know what to do with myself.

It was time to get back to my hosts, in any case, for Christmas lunch. All the way back I was thinking about Rachel, and wondering how to meet her again. I had never been in love before, but I knew for certain that I was now.

I washed in a daze and hurried down to the dining room to eat. The first person I saw at the table was Rachel. For an instant I thought I was hallucinating: perhaps this was what happened when people fell violently in love. I stood and stared at her, feeling weak. Kennedy came up and gravely introduced us.

'Oh, we have met already,' said Rachel. 'Stephen visited us this morning.' I smiled feebly. Throughout that long lunch I barely spoke a word. I was too busy preparing a speech for Rachel. If I say this, will she say that? I asked myself. If I ask her to marry me, what will I do if she says no? I was in real torment. Every so often I'd risk a look at Rachel down the table. She was so beautiful, it made me even more alarmed. It put me right off my food. Never before or since becoming a Christian have I eaten so little at Christmas lunch.

After lunch I asked my hosts if they would mind if I invited Rachel out for a walk. They encouraged us to go ahead, so off we went. Rachel asked me for my story, and I hid nothing – my unhappy childhood in the township, my lack of education, my days with the Youth League, nothing. From her comments: 'Having had no schooling must make you timid,' and, 'I'm sure the nationalists want to change things for the better, but don't know how,' I knew she instinctively understood me and the way I had felt.

By the time we settled on a large rock I knew that this was the only woman in the world for me. We talked some more, and then I decided to tell her.

So without more ado I said, 'I know I've just met you this morning, but I love you already, and it would be the greatest honour if you would be my wife.' Proposing to a girl I had not met until that morning seemed perfectly natural, as I had had those visions which I felt sure were from God.

Rachel was gracious candour itself. 'Thank you for your very big offer,' she said calmly. 'I will have to pray about it – it is a big decision.' She smiled and my heart did several somersaults.

'Yes, of course. Take all the time you need,' I said, and

went back to Zimbabwe with my heart singing. It was enough at present just to be in love. I wrote letters – how I blessed Hannes Joubert for teaching me how to write! – which she answered warmly, but non-committedly.

A year went by. Then in December 1968 I took a bus back to Blantyre, Malawi. I packed my suitcase carefully with all my clothes – I wanted to make as good an impression on Rachel as I could. I had no home or salary to offer her. Nothing but a well-turned-out me.

By the time we reached Blantyre I did not even have that. My suitcase was stolen on the way, and I was left with a Bible and the old travelling clothes I stood up in.

'It's no use,' I lamented. 'I'm done for now. I've got nothing.'

Once in Blantyre I tidied myself up as best I could, and rushed round to Rachel's house. She greeted me with the same warm, kind smile. She was even more beautiful than I remembered. As soon as I could decently get her away from her family, who were a friendly lot, we went for a walk.

We ran out of general conversation pretty quickly. Normally I loved talking about the Dorothea Mission, but the subject seemed unspeakably dull that morning. I was desperate to ask Rachel what her decision was, but was terrified in case it was no. Of course, it had to be no. Why should such a well-educated girl from such a good family, with a job and many local interests, throw it all away for someone like me? My yearning for her and my sense of total inferiority made me almost giddy as we walked along.

'Rachel,' I stammered at last, 'have you thought about. . . .'

She stopped, and I stopped too. She looked up at me gravely and then took a deep breath. 'Yes, Stephen, I have thought.'

Here it was. My future lay in the balance. I gazed down at her. She was so lovely. 'And . . . ?' I stammered at last.

'Yes, Stephen, I will marry you.'

My spirits took off on a roller-coaster of emotions. Up I whizzed to the dizzy heights of sheer elation and joy – and then plunged into the depths of fear and timidity.

'Well, I don't think you'd better,' I stammered. 'Have you thought – it will mean giving up your job, your lovely home, all your friends. And I am a poorly educated man. I will never be able to give you anything.'

'Stephen –,'

'You know I live by faith, but do you realise how simple my lifestyle is?'

'Stephen –,'

'I have no money.'

'Stephen –,'

'I have no house.'

'Stephen –,'

'Or even a bed!'

'Stephen –,'

'Rachel, I haven't even got my suitcase any longer!' A lump rose in my throat. You get attached to the things you own in this world, and to lose them all with the theft of the suitcase had been a shock.

'Stephen –,'

'No, I'm sorry Rachel, I can't possibly marry you. I have nothing.' I felt tied in knots of unworthiness.

At this Rachel burst into a merry peal of laughter. 'Stephen!' She put her finger to my lips. 'Will you listen to me! I am not going to marry a house, bed or clothes. I am going to marry a person. *You.*'

I kissed her finger, I could not help it, but no words came. I choked on my tears. I was looking at a miracle: a woman who loved me just for me. I had surely nothing

else in the world to offer. What a tremendous encouragement to a man like me!

Her family was appalled. They had thought of me as no
more than that nice chap from the Dorothea Mission, the
one with the murky past who had done all sorts of violent
things but who now preached around a bit.

To think of me as a son-in-law was a different matter.
Her uncles were furious. 'Supposing he becomes a nationalist again and wants you to help him throw petrol
bombs?' they demanded.

'I doubt that very much,' Rachel said calmly.

'Didn't you say he lives under a bridge? We don't want
you living under a bridge.'

'He lives with white missionaries now.'

'Supposing he stabs you?'

'Why should he do that, Uncle?'

In the end, it was Rachel's mother who came to our rescue. She had prayed for three years that one of her daughters would marry a pastor. The first had married an econo-
mist, the second a head teacher. That left Rachel. Then I
arrived, not a pastor, but an evangelist. Rachel's mother
was delighted. She accepted my Rhodesian citizenship and
my rough background easily – for her, the fact that I was a
saved man who loved God and preached the gospel was
everything.

I first met her in the living room of Rachel's house. I was
seated on the couch, when her mother came in. 'Mother,'
said Rachel, 'this is Stephen from Rhodesia, the man I told
you about, the man I want to marry.'

In a most un-African display of female affection, her
mother came immediately over to me and knelt before me.
Softly she took my hands in hers and squeezed them. 'Let
us pray,' she whispered. She prayed a prayer of thanks and
welcome for me, until the tears were coursing down my

cheeks. When she finished, she looked deep into my eyes and said, 'You will not be my son-in-law, you will be my *son*.' It was a sublime moment for me which I shall treasure all my life.

Then Rachel's mother sorted out the angry uncles for us. She told them not to worry so much, she knew her daughter was going to be in safe hands.

We decided to get married soon – on 20 December, almost a year to the day after we'd first met.

The family plunged into preparations for the wedding. In my male ignorance I expected this to be pleasant fun, for compared to setting up a Dorothea Mission crusade which involved police and many churches and PA equipment and tents, what could go wrong? Well, to start with, I did not own a suit. (Mine had gone with the suitcase.) Rachel's mother let it be known that without a suit she would hardly consider the marriage to be legal. So my relief was great when, shortly before the wedding, a Christian friend suddenly gave me one of his. I thought all my problems were over.

Then the day before the wedding Rachel's mother realised I had not organised a wedding cake. Had she discovered I was going to petrol-bomb the wedding itself, the alarm and consternation could not have been greater. My frantic pleas: 'But no one told me I needed to provide a cake!' were met with soft murmurs of disdain, little cries of exasperation.

No one believed that even a Rhodesian could be so gauche, so entirely ignorant of wedding etiquette Malawi style. I was so enfeebled by all the looks of sad reproach from the women in the family that I wondered if life would ever again be worth living.

Not only did I not have a cake, I had no money for a cake. So in despair I walked into the bush and prayed.

'Lord,' I said, 'I need money for a wedding cake. I really do. You will embarrass me if I do not get it!'

It was a crazy prayer, but I was under a lot of stress, and desperate. I had no relatives to help me, I was on my own, and God was all I had to turn to for help in getting ready for this marriage. As I returned to the house, someone put an envelope from Salisbury in my hands. I opened it and £80 fell out – just the sum I needed for a wedding cake! (I do not know to this day who sent it to me.)

Anyway, in my innocence, I thought then that my problems were over. I rushed to the local cake shop, to buy a wedding cake. They asked when I wanted it. Right now, I said. They burst into peals of laughter. 'You need to order these things weeks in advance,' the salesgirl said.

In desperation, I tried to buy another sort of cake, but she would not hear of it. 'You cannot possibly serve *that* at a wedding,' she said in scorn.

Crushed, I left the shop. Friday afternoon came and went. I was getting married next day, and still no cake.

After a sleepless night, I returned early the following morning to the cake shop. I passed some people coming out. As I approached the counter, the girls gave me an unexpectedly warm welcome. 'Well, Mr Lungu, you will not believe this, but do you know who those people were who passed you just now?'

'Who?' I asked blankly.

'They were people who had ordered a large wedding cake for this morning, and they have just been in to cancel it. So – if you want it, you can have your wedding cake after all!'

I heaved a great sigh of joyous relief. My wedding was going to be a success after all! 'Thank you God, thank you God,' was all I could think.

The cake was safely delivered to the uncles to take to the

wedding reception, and I arrived early at the church. I gave a great sigh of relief. My suit was on, the cake was ready to be eaten. I'd finally made it, and this was my wedding morning. I stood outside in the hot sunshine, chatting happily with the ushers, and then noticed that my best man was looking a bit peaky. We went into the church at the start of the service, and waited up at the front for the bride to arrive. Suddenly, my best man collapsed. He was being carried off to hospital just as Rachel and her parents arrived at the church!

There was a moment of horror when I feared that Rachel's uncles would now think I'd been attacking the wedding guests. But the minister smoothed things over and, much to my surprise, managed to marry us before anything else went wrong.

Our honeymoon was spent in Salima, and the early weeks of our marriage were spent in a small house in Blantyre belonging to one of Rachel's sisters. Housekeeping was minimal; the house only measured seven feet by seven feet and our bed took up more than half the space. We stored our things in a new suitcase (a wedding present) under the bed.

We found that the biggest challenge in our new life together was simply getting in and out of the house. The door opened inwards, and half way in it hit the bed, leaving about two square feet of houseroom free for standing in. So if Rachel was inside and I was outside, and she wanted to be outside and I to be inside, we found it was best achieved by the following method: Rachel would perch on the bed, and open the door. I would edge in, and climb on the bed beside her. Then she would climb down, and edge out of the door.

But within days I wasn't going anywhere – I had succumbed to malaria (Malawi is worse for this than

Zimbabwe) and Rachel very nearly lost me.

As soon as they could get me mobile I was packed off home to Salisbury, and Rachel followed shortly afterwards. Patrick and Hannes Joubert had found a new home for us near the Dorothea Mission compound. It was nearly nine feet square, which meant we could get the bed as well as a small table inside, and even both of us standing up inside at the same time.

Rachel brought me greater love and joy than I would ever have thought possible. She was everything any man could ever want in a woman: a loving wife, a mother, a sister, a friend. I thanked God every day for her, and could still hardly believe she had been willing to leave her family and secure job to marry me.

As I grew to know her better, I also learned what an anchor God had given me in her. She became my secure and quiet hiding place; a haven of peace and tranquillity at the centre of my life.

It was also, I have to admit, a sheer delight to have someone interested in my daily welfare. Rachel was an accomplished cook and seamstress. She fed me glorious meals and patched my trousers and darned my socks faster than I had been able to thread the needle. I put on weight, and never left the house looking less than immaculate. This was noticed at the Dorothea Mission, where they warmed to her evident love for me, and then to her own gentle ways.

She was also a knowledgeable woman. Sometimes I would watch her in company, holding her own in discussion about the political and economic situation with Patrick, Johannes and the other white missionaries, and it would arouse such admiration in me that it turned to fear.

One night in particular, I had a complete crisis of confidence. Patrick had told me off for something, and then enjoyed a long chat with Rachel, as with an equal. We left for home with me in the doldrums. My heart was too heavy to respond to Rachel's happy chatter. I almost regretted marrying her: why had I aimed so high? Could I keep her love? In marrying Rachel I felt I had set myself up for certain failure.

Rachel had gone quiet too, and then her slim fingers reached for my hand. 'What is wrong, Stephen?'

There was no hiding from Rachel – she would never let me brood. As soon as she had coaxed the problem out of me, she set about making it better. She gently rebuked me: she could have had her choice of well-to-do bank managers, but she had wanted me, and had had no illusions about the simplicity of our lifestyle.

This was just as well, as sometimes we ran out of food. The first time it happened, I'd just returned from a mission and was looking forward to a hot meal.

'There wasn't anything left to cook, Stephen, I'm sorry,' my wife said calmly. I felt terrible. It was my job to provide, and she was apologising to me for no food. Fighting down panic that my dear wife would go hungry, I tried to set a Christian manly example: 'Let's pray for it. God knows I have been working for him this past week. I am sure he will provide for us now.'

Rachel had not been asked to pray for food before, and I wondered how she'd take it. She was magnificent. We said a simple prayer, and then she began to move about the room.

'What are you doing?'

She glanced at me in surprise. 'Setting the table.'

I gulped and looked at this diminutive woman in awe. Here was a comrade for life!

Two hours passed. Then came a knock at our door. We rushed to open it together and saw a pair of legs, and two stringy arms clutching two huge bags of food. Two eyes peeped merrily at us over the top of the bags. A friend from church.

'I was praying about you this morning, and I felt I must bring you some food and money. I meant to come earlier, but I got delayed.'

At other times we needed clothes, and quietly, undramatically, trousers and dresses would be provided. It would be hard to say how we survived, but we did. There was a series of small, everyday, casual miracles, performed by people who loved us, who supported my work with the Dorothea Mission, and who believed they could have a share in this important evangelistic ministry by supporting the full-time workers.

Such finances as we had, Rachel took over – she had worked for Barclays Bank, and as such was the banker in our family. The local women were profoundly impressed. An African woman with access to her husband's money? General consensus: she had given me some black magic. They begged and begged her for the recipe so that they could stop their husbands drinking every penny they earned.

Rachel's new friends were incredulous when all she produced was the Bible. But Rachel loved to share her faith in Christ, and delighted in explaining Christianity to the women. She won many ladies to the Lord in this way. Then they would pray for their husbands and introduce me to them, and I would tell them what had happened to me. Many of the husbands decided to become Christians. Rachel and I did not know it then, but this cottage-style joint evangelism and marriage counselling would feature large in our future.

When our first child, Agnes, named after Shadrach's wife, arrived, Patrick astounded me by firmly pointing out that it was my job to help Rachel care for the baby.

'But women care for babies!'

'Rachel is not your slave or your housekeeper. She is part of you – and you must show the love that Christ showed us.'

So I helped to wash the nappies and shared the job of walking the floor at night. I was no New Man and found it hard work. It kept Rachel and me very close, and gave me a chance to really delight in my daughter. I was determined she would have a happier, better childhood than I had ever known. The love my father and mother had not been able to give me, I wanted to give to my own children.

I had not really thought about my parents in years, but having a baby certainly brought home to me again how I had a family of my own somewhere – and they had a grand-daughter, if only they knew. But they had deserted me. Odd how the old ache was still there.

Meanwhile, of course, the work of the Dorothea Mission team went on.

It was a changed team, though, because even before I had married Rachel, Patrick had married and brought Jill into our lives. I suppose I had slightly dreaded her arrival. Patrick was a born leader, and could be forceful and brisk if the occasion demanded it. Would Jill be a female Patrick? Even worse, would she drive a wedge between Patrick and me because I was black? Some missionaries were very 'paternalistic'.

Within an hour of meeting her, my fears had vanished like smoke. Jill was a charming, gracious, gentle woman who had worked in Africa for several years, and had a great love for black people. From the day I met her I loved her, and my only regret was that she had not been married to Patrick for years and years.

She rapidly became the soothing buffer for the team

whenever tensions arose. I would often quarrel with Patrick, but never with Jill. The way she'd approach any contentious issue would melt me completely. Such love. She was a sympathetic, caring woman who was so diplomatic that I would have cheerfully done anything in the world for her.

There was only one thing that amazed me: watching Jill and Patrick together. My first view of European marriage was culturally bewildering to me.

They treated each other with such familiarity. Patrick flatly contradicted Jill at times, and Jill told Patrick not to be a silly idiot at other times. In Africa, this would have caused mortal offence. But each would casually apologise, or look sheepish, and a few minutes later they'd be laughing over something else. The other thing that astonished me was the caring concern which Patrick showed to Jill. Her life was that of a queen compared to most African women. It made a great impression on me, and helped guide my own behaviour towards Rachel.

Patrick and Jill still had a little thirteen-foot caravan that Patrick had acquired some years before. It had been a home away from home when we evangelists had gone on missions around the country. Jill's delicious meals done on a 'steam pot' during those busy days of evangelising were a great boost to our energy. Our shared laughter and talk in that caravan at the end of long days of mission remain one of the happier memories in my life. This, I felt, was how a marriage and life should be.

Another major change for the Dorothea Mission team was that by this time Patrick had been asked to compile a handbook for Christians wanting to pray for mission throughout the world. *Operation World* would become an international best-seller, but that was still some years in the future. With my shorter-sighted view of things, I could only puzzle as to why Patrick wasted so much time during the afternoons scribbling away in the van instead of accompanying us out and about, visiting people.

Patrick's slight withdrawal from leadership was of course all part of his ten-year plan to prepare us Africans for leadership. It was now the early 1970s, and he felt it was high time for me to start organising things.

Oh my goodness!

One morning Patrick sat back from the breakfast table and gave me his considering look, which I always found dangerous. But this time I did not see what could possibly go wrong.

'We can have some more meetings whenever you like, Stephen.'

I did not see the trap and walked straight into it. 'Let's try Mpopoma township then – I know there is interest there!'

'Fine. This time you are going to do the organising.'

I was appalled. 'What!'

'You are going to do the organising for this mission you want at Mpopoma township.'

Panic set in right away. 'No, no, no! I will never be able to . . . to write letters and see the police and talk to church-es . . . .' I was aghast at the very thought. 'I am not educat-ed.'

'Yes you are – what do you think I have been teaching you all these years?'

'I don't know.' I bit my lip stubbornly.

'Stephen, you can do it.'

'No.'

'Yes.'

'No.'

'Yes!'

I knew that tone of voice and my heart sank.

'I am an evangelist, not an organiser,' I told my pillow that night. 'He is a harsh man.'

'We begin with the letter to the police,' said Patrick next morning. 'Write the letter, Stephen.'

'They will not want to hear from a black man.'

'Write it!'

'I can't'

'You can.'

I wrote it. Slowly and laboriously I wrote that letter.

'This is terrible!' he tore it up.

'I told you! You must write it.'

'No. I'll show you what is wrong and you can copy what I write.'

So I copied what he wrote. He tore it up.

'You tore it up!'

'Well, I could not read it!'

'He is a harsh man,' I reminded my pillow that night.

Next morning we tried again. Hours later a letter of sorts from me to the police was ready.

'Now take it to the police,' said Patrick.

'Not by myself,' I wailed.

'Yes.'

'They want white people.'

'No. You go. You go and tell them.' Patrick added some advice: 'Don't chitchat. Get to the point. Forget the weather. Forget the flowers.' He knew my African tendency to approach things by running in circles around them. 'Say exactly what you want. At the beginning.'

Instead I stuttered, and forgot all the English I ever knew and hung my head.

The police said no.

I came home almost in tears. 'They said no.'

'Go back and insist!'

'Harsh man, harsh man,' I muttered as I dragged myself

all the way back.

This time I was so obviously terrified that the District Commissioner must have had pity on me, and gave in.

'He said yes!'

Patrick smiled and patted my shoulder. A smile from him lit up my day. I felt so weak with relief that I had to sit down and have some tea. Thus Patrick squeezed out my inferiority complex.

The mission passed off without any due upsets, and I found that I had this job of preparation forced on me many times. I objected violently at first, but Patrick refused to budge. Time and again, the police granted my requests, much to my amazement. I slowly got used to visiting the police station and then to organising other aspects of the missions while Patrick sat in his van and wrote his book.

Then one Sunday afternoon, just when I'd thought things were going well (Patrick hadn't told me off for a few days), disaster struck.

We had just settled ourselves down at the table for one of Jill's wonderful Sunday lunches and I had carefully pulled my chair up to the table, remembered to offer Jill the vegetables first, and was gently coaxing some potatoes onto my plate with a spoon while sitting upright and keeping my elbows at my sides and my feet on the floor, when Patrick suddenly announced: 'Oh Steve, I have a message from Pastor B for you.' Pastor B headed up a large, white, English-speaking Baptist church in Bulawayo, where Patrick had preached that morning. 'He wants you to come and preach at his church two weeks from today.'

'What!' I jerked the spoon and the potatoes bounced onto the white tablecloth. Patrick winced and sighed.

'You are invited to preach at the Baptist church in two weeks. I said you'd be glad to.'

'Oh.' I was stunned. Jill quietly rounded up the potatoes.

'Well, if you're translating for me, you'll have to understand my Shona. Perhaps when I have written the sermon
we can have several trial runs of you translating it before
we go . . . .'

Patrick cut through my nervous, half-formed plans as he
reached for the yams. 'No way. The time has come for you
to preach to white people in English.'

I was appalled. 'No! I preach in Shona.'

'You preach in English.' Patrick said slowly and with
finality. Then he calmly ate his lunch.

I could manage barely a mouthful, and after the dishes
were washed and put away, I went for a restless walk.
Preaching in English did not bear thinking about. I certainly could not bear to think about it. I *would* not think about
it. By the time I returned from my walk I had decided that
Patrick must be joking.

I spent a harrowing ten days working on a Shona sermon, carefully and laboriously written and rewritten. It
took hours and hours, all of them unhappy. The thought of
a large white congregation terrified me.

Patrick watched me suffering and writing and chewing
the end of my pencil, but made no comment, and did not
ask to see what I was doing.

Until the Friday before my big day. Then instead of our
usual lessons, Patrick said: 'Come on, Steve, let's see your
sermon.'

I was moderately pleased with it by now, and brought it
over for approval. There was only a slight niggle in my
mind: that he might notice it was in Shona after all, and
not English. Patrick took it from me, and leafed through it
rapidly with a grave face. I held my breath. Then suddenly
he tore my sermon into shreds.

'No!' I wailed, utterly aghast.

'Stephen, you are preaching in English.'

Saturday I spent fasting, praying and crying to God. 'Lord, this man is very, very, very hard and unfair. He has put me in an awful position. He is determined to embarrass me.'

On Saturday evening Jill came to me in my desolation. 'Stephen, I am praying for you, and I will be praying for you all the way through that service tomorrow.' She laid a gentle hand on my shoulder. As always, it worked magic. I felt encouraged by her warmth.

Next morning at the Baptist church the pastor took one look at my stricken face and piled on the reassurance as well. 'Stephen, I am sure you will do splendidly. I have told my folk a bit about you, and they are anxious to hear your story. My people will be blessed by your testimony.'

The church was packed. I sat miserably on the platform while the service got under way. My time came. The pastor summoned me to the lectern and placed the microphone around my neck like a noose. The Bible shook in my hands and my knees felt weak. I spotted Patrick and Jill in the congregation and their heads were bowed in prayer.

'Oh God, help,' I prayed, and I plunged in. I have no memory of how I started, and I knew I was stammering and often at a loss for words. Then suddenly I found myself at the bit in my story where I was holding my petrol bombs and walking down the aisle. The memory of the old burning, longing for God came back to me and I tried as best I could to explain this to the congregation. I then went on to tell them about my days of preaching on the buses and finding Johannes and then Patrick. By then I had really used up all my English, so I sat down.

Silence reigned in the congregation. Then to my surprise I heard quiet, stifled sobs. Some folk in the congregation were crying! I was astonished. I had never even seen whites cry before.

The pastor picked up the threads of the service and graciously thanked me, but I was too euphoric to do anything but sit there in a daze of relief that it was over.

Afterwards back home, Patrick chaired a 'Debriefing of the First Sermon in English'. On the minus side, he and Jill had filled three pages of mistakes I had made in grammar and vocabulary. Gently they took me through these, explaining where I'd gone wrong.

'Now, as to the plus side, Stephen,' Patrick said, 'your content was good. These white people understood your message and what it was you were trying to say. You have the ability to communicate, and your love for the Lord and desire to tell the gospel are self-evident. You did well!'

This was high praise indeed from Patrick, and I was jubilant.

I thought of the young man who'd come up to me in tears afterwards. If I'd been able to get him to think about God, then I was well satisfied.

In the meantime, Patrick handed me the Monday English newspaper: 'Here, you go, Stephen, here's another daily dose of English for you . . . .'

Though incidents like the Baptist church were traumatic, Patrick was simply taking any opportunity to try and help me grow. He knew more clearly than I the sort of experience and skills I needed to acquire if I was to make the most of my calling to evangelism.

The first half of the 1970s would see a great surge in church growth in Africa, and it was a privilege to work alongside Christians throughout central and southern Africa, helping them to evangelise needy people. Everywhere, from Zambia to Botswana, the cities were teaming with life, but people were so lost. They had such need for stability and faith in God. Political turmoil was everywhere. Many times as I stood to speak to hundreds or even thousands of people at our open-air crusades, I would be reminded of the words of Jesus: 'The fields are ready for harvest. Ask the Lord of the harvest to send out workers.'

I was willing to go anywhere he sent me.

CHAPTER FIFTEEN

MOTHER

One day Patrick and Hannes Joubert sent a message asking me to come for a meeting to the Bible school office. I went over early, because first I had a few choice words of my own to share with the students. They had been helping me on one of the local crusades, and I was not impressed.

I found them in the sunshine outside, and soon darkened their day for them. When I get angry, I go black as midnight.

I sailed right in: 'Last night's meeting was a disgrace, and you know it. Some of you were half an hour late. What sort of behaviour is that!

'The police told me that you hadn't been accurate about expected crowd numbers or the location of the tent . . . someone put out half-filled paraffin lamps . . . the chairs were still wet . . . and if you call that a PA system, we may as well use hollow cow horns and be done with it.

'As for the worship,' I went on, 'I've got aunts who sounded more cheerful than that when they once thought I was dead! Not to mention the piano – why wasn't it made into firewood weeks ago?

'Now tonight I want to see a vast improvement, or know

the reason why not!'

The students hung their heads in contrition, and I stormed off to my own meeting, realising a moment later that I had left something behind.

I headed back for it, but just as I reached the doorway, I heard one tell the others: 'Oh, Stephen Lungu is far worse than Mr Johnstone. Stephen is so particular – everything has to be just so.'

'Yeah,' agreed his friend. 'When I saw you come in late, I knew you'd be for it. One minute late with Stephen, and you are dog's meat.'

'He didn't really expect me to contradict the police, did he?'

'He's very firm with them at times – just like the English.'

'He even sounds English,' sighed another.

Then they wandered off, leaving me too stunned to move. Memories of Patrick and me and all our battles filled me, and my sudden peals of laughter swept through the house. I was still grinning when I wandered in to see Patrick and Hannes.

'Ah, Stephen – you look in top form. Good, because we have an idea we want to put to you.'

Enthusiastically they outlined their latest plan, and within a few minutes I was a quivering wreck. It was as well that the students could not see me now.

'You want me to *what?*'

'Come to Mozambique with Patrick and me,' said Hannes Joubert. 'Be our spokesman when we approach the governor of Beira.' He was part of the new independent government, and in charge of the region where we wanted to hold a mission. Following the communist revolution there, the country was in some confusion, but might well offer an opportunity for evangelism. But the political situation was so sensitive that only blacks would be safe in leading missions within the country. So the plan was for Patrick and Hannes Joubert to help me behind the scenes in Salisbury, but for me to lead two teams into Mozambique.

I sighed bitterly. Just when I thought I had done and achieved everything anyone could possibly ask of me, these two friends of mine would set me at a fence which looked absolutely impossible to me. It never cheered me up to think that I had thought that about many jobs they had given me in the past but which nowadays I did without thinking twice.

'I will feel uncomfortable on such an important visit,' I pleaded. I felt my old insecurities sweeping over me. 'People will ask me who I think I am, and they will be right. Someone with more education should go with you. This is too high for me.'

Patrick lifted an eyebrow. 'Where,' he said mildly, 'have I heard this before?' And I knew all my arguments were lost. As long as I worked with Patrick, I would always be his disciple. Every time I achieved anything, he would use it as a new departure to push me towards something new. 'You have great leadership ability, Stephen,' was his argument, 'and you must learn how to develop it.'

So off we went in 1975 to Mozambique. It was the start, if only we had known, of five years of intensive persecution of Christians in that country. But we did not know. We managed to secure an audience with the all-important governor of Beira, in the eastern part of the country. Patrick was adamant that it was I who should do the talking.

'You know as well as we do what we want.'

So with fear and literal trembling I was our spokesman to the governor, the police and other top government officials. How glad I was no Dorothea Mission students could hear my stammerings now!

Briefly I stated my case: we were Christians who would like to visit their country from time to time to hold missions alongside local churches. Our aim was to make more Christians who would then become part of the Christian church of Mozambique. Christians were good and faithful citizens who would help promote stability and good living among their neighbours. Would this be OK?

The officials seemed pleasantly surprised that I was the spokesman, and promised us no official hassle – and indeed support.

Once back in Salisbury, I quickly organised and led a team of eight Dorothea missioners back to Beira. What a response from the people! The team was deeply moved to see how God had touched so many hearts, and how people came forward for more help.

On the Sunday some soldiers drove up to watch us preach in the open air. We smiled at them. They promptly arrested us. This seemed a bit much, and I protested noisily. A soldier hit me, hard, and I shut up.

He pointed to our truck: a 'Buffalo Body' made in South Africa. 'You are spies.'

'No. The truck has been given to us so we can come and preach the gospel.'

'Yes, and then spy on us. Give us your documents.'

But I had changed after church and had left our documents in my suit. My heart sank. Patrick and Hannes Joubert would never have been so careless. I explained the problem as best I could: 'If you will take us to where we are staying, I will show you our papers.'

They brutally refused, and threw us into their van. At the police station we were beaten, their rifle butts smashing toes and arches, an agonising procedure. They flung us to the floor of the reception area, and left us moaning in great pain. I felt, however irrationally, that if we died, it would be all my fault. I flung myself on God's mercy. Only he could help us now.

Some hours later there was a change of guard and, lo and behold, a soldier appeared who had been converted at one of our meetings the previous day. He was horrified.

'What are you doing here?'

We explained. He rushed to his superiors and vouched for us. 'They are preaching.'

The superiors almost apologised. 'These are troubled days for our country,' they said, and released us.

A Christian doctor bandaged us up and we carried on. The rest of that six-week mission was a great success.

Ironically, it was at a local mission in Salisbury in 1976 that I received the greatest surprise of my entire preaching career.

I was working with a Dorothea Mission team in a mission in Gillingham township. It had been a long day of no less than six open-air meetings, and I was exhausted with preaching. Hoarsely, I wound up the evening tent meeting, and made a most uninspired invitation for anyone interested to come forward.

To my surprise, several people did, and my helpers came quietly forward to talk with them. I unhooked the mike and was turning away from the platform, longing for a cool drink, when someone clutched at my trouser leg. I looked down. A little woman was standing in front of the platform, looking up at me.

I crouched down to have a better look at her. She was a bit of a mess. She was thin, looked ill and stank of alcohol. She was drunk.

'I would like to pray with you,' she said abruptly, staring at me in the most peculiar way.

'Well, *Mai* (in Shona, women are all addressed as ''moth-

er"), I am exhausted, and would not like to pray with you,'
I thought uncharitably, but said instead, 'Why not talk
with one of our women counsellors?' I felt bone weary and
quite unready for a major counselling session.

'I already have. Now I want you to pray with me.'

So I left the platform, and came and knelt down to pray
with her. It was the only way I could get her to let go of my
trouser leg. At least she meant business with God, because
the Lord touched her, and she began jumping about and
saying her pain was gone.

Pain? What pain? I began to wake up a little in spite of
myself. Then she wanted to accept Jesus and become a
Christian.

I was touched by her excitement, so I knelt again and we
prayed again. This time she wanted to pray as well, and
once started she went on and on. And on. I could catch
hardly a word of her high-pitched stream, and soon fatigue
swept over me again. I slumped wearily against the lectern
while she babbled away to her new-found heavenly Father.
I longed to go home, but could not feel impatient: the miracle of a wretched human soul finding peace with God
could never lose its enchantment for me. The delight and
wonder of it touched me as it always did. Finally she
turned to me, and I smiled in spite of my tiredness at her
joy.

'Why not come back tomorrow night,' I suggested. She
had now attached her fingers to my sleeve, and I was trying to disentangle myself. She obviously needed help. I
would make sure some sympathetic woman counsellor
was again on hand to help her tomorrow night.

Then abruptly: 'Do you know you are my son?'

I smiled. I was well used to the idea of 'spiritual families', though she had got it wrong. 'I am now your father in
God,' I corrected her gently.

'No, no, no, you are my son,' she croaked. 'I am your mother.'

I looked at her. Deep into her eyes.

She looked at me. 'Back in Highfield,' she said. 'You and your brother John and sister Malesi. From what you said tonight, I know I was – am – your mother.'

Her words sunk in at last, and I felt the shock of it hit me like a physical force. The years peeled away and I relived the terror of that dreadful day. This small, shrivelled-up, ill lady was the glossy, round young woman that had abandoned my sister, my brother and me to probable death twenty years ago. I had not seen her since that terrible day when as a young teenager I had found her outside Aunt M's kitchen, and thrown a knife at her. How much we had both changed!

I stared and stared. So here was Mother at last. My mother. Nearly twenty years since I had last spoken with her. In a palpable wave the hurt and bitterness of that separation swept over me. Why, why, why? All those years! All those years of misery and hunger. I could have starved to death as a child, died of disease or exposure for all she had seemed to care.

'Oh, God!' I cried inside, as I realised something with shock: 'I still hate my own mother!' I thought I had forgiven her years ago.

Then, deep inside me, far off, as if from a different world, I heard a compassionate voice say, 'Accept her. She has found me through you – she is your mother. Now she needs you. Do not abandon her.'

The woman certainly needed help. She told me that she was living nearby, but that her present husband, a Muslim, was beating her badly. She was scared and in constant pain from the blows. So I agreed to meet her the following day, **and went home in a daze.**

Rachel took one look at my face. 'Stephen! What is wrong?'

I sat down heavily on the bed and buried my face in my hands. And broke into sobs.

'My dear, you are ill! What is it!' She was badly alarmed.

'Rachel, I . . . '

'What?'

'Rachel. My . . . ' I could not say it. My dear wife knelt before me and cradled me in her arms.

'Stephen, what?'

'My – mother.'

'Your mother? What about her?'

'I've found her.'

'What! Is she dead?'

'She came to the meeting tonight.'

'Oh, Stephen!'

If ever I loved Rachel, it was in the weeks that followed. Though heavily pregnant, my saint of a wife welcomed my prodigal mother as if she were the Queen of England, and gave her a home with us. She deloused and de-fleaed her, washed her, burned her clothes, found her fresh ones, kept her off the beer; fed her, and alerted the ladies in the church that their friendship would soon be needed.

Under such treatment my mother progressed rapidly. I smiled and nodded, but kept out of her way as best I could. I felt awkward around her. I was dying to ask her why she had left me, and where she had gone. But I could not bring myself to ask her. The pain of rejection rose again and again in my throat.

How could I say, 'Oh, by the way, remember that time when I was about seven and you took me and my brother and sister into town and told us to wait a minute for you? You never came back – not in twenty years. What kept you? In the following weeks and months and years, did you just forget us? Did you ever worry about us? Did you care at all?'

No. I could not ask. My pain would make me too vulnerable. I could not cope with such defencelessness.

Some weeks into her stay with us, my mother and I sat outside the house, enjoying the late afternoon sunshine. We got talking and suddenly we were into her past. She was still frightened of her present husband. 'When did you marry him?' I ventured, keeping my voice carefully neutral.

She was vague. 'It was after I got back from Bulawayo.'

'Bulawayo!' I exclaimed involuntarily.

'Yes.'

'What were you doing there?'

'I had some friends. We were brewing beer.'

'Brewing beer?' I stared at her in astonishment.

She seemed embarrassed now, and added in a very small voice. 'That's where I went after . . . after . . .'

That was all. So now I knew. We sat in silence for a while.

'My mother abandoned us on the streets of Salisbury to go and brew beer in Bulawayo!' I whispered my anguish to Rachel in bed that night. I wept in her arms. She soothed me as best she could.

'There must be more to it, Stephen, there must be. Remember, she was but a child herself at the time, and had not wanted to marry your father. She was a victim too. Remember that. She had nowhere to go. She is to be pitied very much.'

In later years, medical friends would tell me about clinical depression. They would tell me that my mother's forced marriage at thirteen to a man she did not love, and three children in quick succession could easily have triggered a major depression and despair in her. But at the time I could not understand my mother.

My inner anguish began to affect my work. One night I was preaching on forgiveness when I suddenly choked. Who was I to tell anyone the Christian line, when I now knew that a great part of me still hated my mother? I wanted to forgive her, but simply could not. The knowledge swept over me like a flood of absolute despair, and I began to weep. I wound up the meeting quickly – and excused myself from the team.

'I'm not well Patrick, I need to get away.'

With exquisite sensitivity, he let me go with a soothing, 'Yes of course, we can manage here.'

He had been talking to Rachel about me, and was concerned.

I fled into the night, and did what many Africans do in times of great trouble – I sought solace in the deep bush. For three days I wandered in the wilderness in great turmoil of spirit. I fasted and prayed endlessly. I cried to God to heal me of all the wounds that the rejection and loneliness and fears of my childhood had caused me. I wanted to forgive my mother completely, and to let go of this burden of pain.

'God,' I wept, 'I must forgive her. How can I ever preach again about your love and forgiveness unless I do?'

On the third day I had a strange and marvellous experience. I suddenly felt that God was lifting the weight of hate and resentment from me, as I could not do it myself. I felt the bitterness give way to compassionate feelings for a helpless 'old' woman. I saw my mother as if from God's viewpoint: a poor, helpless, hurting soul. And I could love her now. My inner healing was at last becoming complete. I was no longer an emotional cripple.

After this I returned to Rachel, my mother, and evangelism with the Dorothea Mission. I had a great surge of energy for this work of spreading the good news of the kingdom of God. It meant more to me than anything else in the world, except Rachel. The late 1970s saw a surge of church growth across Africa, and I rushed about central and southern Africa, knee-deep in teams and tents and crowds and campaigns, and the joy of seeing people's lives changed as they discovered the love of God for themselves.

The late 1970s were a fruitful period for my family as well. After two years, we found my mother a little house of her own nearby in Gillingham, for we needed more space: our daughter Agnes was followed by two more children. When a niece of mine had an unwanted child, we took that child in as well. Our family was growing rapidly.

My mother grew in her Christian faith in the most marvellous way. In time, she applied and was accepted at the Soteria Bible School. She studied hard for three years, and I was enormously proud of her. Then she became an evangelist as well, specialising in children's mission and women's meetings. It was lovely to see how finding God had brought her so much fulfilment and happiness, after all the heartbreak in her life. I took special pleasure in sharing the platform with her at some of our campaigns. I got a kick out of introducing her as *my* spiritual daughter. These were happy and blessed times indeed. (For two years my mother was even transferred to Zambia to work with the Dorothea Mission team there. Nothing like having two international evangelists in the same family. Like son, like mother!)

CHAPTER SIXTEEN

BACK TO MALAWI

In 1978 Patrick Johnstone and the Dorothea Mission leaders from South Africa summoned me to a meeting. They wanted me to talk to them about Malawi – how did I assess it in terms of our Dorothea Mission ministry?

I waxed warm on the subject: I loved Malawi. I was half Malawian myself, and my wife was Malawian. I felt it was my second country. It was a much poorer country than Zimbabwe, the political repression hampered even Christian outreach at times, but still I loved to take missions there. I had made many friends in my visits over the years, and they helped make the work so worth while. People were spiritually receptive, and the churches really co-operated, and welcomed in any new converts we made.

Fine, said the Dorothea Mission Board. So what did I think of the idea of opening a small, permanent Dorothea Mission presence there by beginning a Malawi team?

I thought it a wonderful idea. 'The need is there, but the ground is well prepared. I would love to work with such a team.' I was daydreaming out loud.

'How would you like to launch and lead such a team?'

I gasped. For once I was really speechless. Never before

had a black African led a Dorothea Mission national team. It just had not been done. To be asked now was the greatest honour imaginable.

Patrick caught my eye. Only he knew what this offer, this supreme vote of confidence, would mean to me. The Dorothea Mission, being South African based, was very conservative. The whites were considered the unquestioned leaders. Anything else was unheard of. Until now.

The ensuing busyness and excitement in the Lungu household had to be seen to be believed. Rachel was radiant at the thought of living near her family and showing off the grandchildren. I rejoiced with her, but as the moving day approached, I felt a wrench at my heart-strings: I was leaving such family as I had and above all Patrick and Jill. (Hannes Joubert had moved on to new work in South Africa by this time.)

As always, whenever I wanted real sympathy I went to Jill. 'You are and always will be part of our family, but it is time that you put all this training into proper use and started a work in Malawi,' she said.

'I knew you could do it, Steve,' Patrick grinned wickedly, remembering all my howls of protest down the years.

'But what will I do without you?' I grieved.

'You'll do fine. Trust your judgement. And anyway, we will not be here much longer.' After many many years in Africa, Patrick and Jill felt God was calling them back to England to a new work.

'No. I know – I'll simply imagine you into the situation and then do exactly what you'd do!' We laughed. My imitation of Patrick was legendary in the mission.

I loved them both dearly. No one knew better than I that God had given this dear white brother the enormous task of making something of me. Anything I would ever become or achieve would be entirely due to his marvellous dedication to me. Patrick would disagree with this, telling me that I had had all the natural ability and leadership talent from the start – he was just helping me to discover it within myself.

Anyway, I said yes to opening a new team in Malawi. But never mind putting the new Dorothea Mission in Malawi on the map – we needed just to get on the road. A generous Christian in South Africa obliged, and soon Rachel, all the children and I were crammed into a VW Beetle with all our worldly belongings, chugging off to take Malawi by storm.

We made our base in Blantyre, at Rachel's mother's home (her father was long dead). To be precise, we were given a room in which we had a bed, our belongings and our children. Some slept with us in the bed, and the smaller ones slept under the bed.

I had many Christian contacts in Malawi. My first job was to let them know I'd come back to stay.

I was invited to preach at many churches and church meetings. I explained that the Dorothea Mission saw its work as a handmaiden to the local churches – helping it with evangelism and therefore growth by holding missions and crusades in markets, factories, schools or wherever. Our policy was never to build our own churches, but to feed converts into the local churches.

The Malawi Christians were wonderful, and gave me a splendid welcome wherever I went, promising financial support and helpers. Several booked me up for missions, and before I knew it, the work was underway. I revelled in the missions – to which hundreds and up to several thousands would come. How much easier it was to plan and hold them from our own base in Blantyre rather than attempting it from Salisbury.

When the rainy season arrived, and open-air crusades

were impossible, Rachel and I looked for opportunities for Christian outreach closer to home. When local Christians in the townships round about Blantyre launched home Bible-study groups, they began to invite Rachel and I to come and share with them. We accepted gladly. People came out of curiosity, and seemed to enjoy hearing what we had learned over the years. The groups grew quickly, so we established a rule: no more than twenty could come. When any group reached twenty, it must split in half and meet in a new part of the town. Within months this simple network of groups was mushrooming, pulling in hundreds of local Christians and interested non-believers.

Of course, even in the rainy season it did not rain all the time, and it was good to slip out for a breath of air in the evening. This led us by accident to a new form of evangelism – our homespun open-air meetings. They began when our Bible study group sat outside our house one evening and began singing choruses for fun. Soon, to our amazement, folk began drifting out of their homes and coming over to see what was happening – they were bored with the rain, too.

Soon we had a relaxed and receptive crowd, just waiting for something to happen. I couldn't resist it: I stood up and gave a simple testimony as to why I was singing with joy, and several people became Christians. Gleefully, the Dorothea Mission (Malawi) team resolved to use and tell others of this low-key approach – evangelism without leaving your own front garden!

Three very happy years went by with missions throughout Malawi and Rhodesia, which in 1980 had become Zimbabwe. We welcomed any Dorothea Mission visitors, and delighted in sharing news of our progress. Our converts ranged from simple folk to commercial bankers and even a football commentator for the Malawi Broadcasting Corporation.

Soon, thanks to the generosity of local Christians, I was able to take on two more workers and buy them little houses. Rachel and I were so used to managing with children in one room that we did not dream of moving out. Well, I did briefly, but hesitated: I was used to managing with little and did not want to discourage my workers by having better housing than they. But another child had arrived by now, and even I at times felt that seven of us in one room was a bit much.

Then late in the spring of 1981, a Keswick Convention was held in Malawi, bringing together thousands of Christians. I loved these big conventions, and looked forward to hearing the guest speakers.

To my delight, I was asked if I would translate for one of them, a Michael Cassidy from South Africa. Everyone had heard of him – he was the founder of African Enterprise – big boys compared to the little Dorothea Mission. AE had enormous resources compared with us, because they had support from several thousand Christians in America, Canada, Australia and New Zealand.

The Keswick organiser thanked me for my willingness: 'You see, Mr Cassidy wanted someone absolutely fluent in English, with a real flair for language.' I nodded graciously, and smothered a grin. Patrick should be here now!

The night arrived, and I stood up on the platform beside Michael Cassidy. He began to preach. It took me about a minute to decide that this guy was great stuff. It was natural for me to fall in with his urgency, to let the same passion for winning souls show in my voice, and soon without realising it, I was waving my arms about in emphatic support of what I said. Soon we were thundering along together, our styles in marvellous harmony. Even so, he was astonished to find his interpreter turning an interpretation into a sermon in its own right. He came up to me afterwards with a friendly, disarming grin, and stated the obvious: 'I see you are an evangelist!'

'Oh yes!' We chatted a bit, and then he wanted me to show him the national HQ of Dorothea Mission in Malawi. This was a bit embarrassing, but I drove him back to my mother-in-law's and explained that the HQ was one room which doubled as home for my children, my wife and myself, and that it would be more peaceful to stay in the car.

Michael Cassidy looked startled, and then intrigued. He questioned me closely about the mission, and then about myself. 'How did you become a Christian yourself?' he wanted to know. So, sitting cramped in a small white VW Beetle outside the house, I told him, feeling, as always, slightly ashamed of my background. This man had been to Cambridge University.

He sat in silence for a while when I had finished and I saw him wipe his eyes. 'Brother, where have you taken this ministry of yours?'

I hadn't thought of it that way before. I merely listed the places I had preached: South Africa, Zambia, Mozambique, Malawi, and of course, Zimbabwe. Say central and southern Africa and you'd sum it up.

Michael Cassidy shook his head slowly. 'No, no. That is fine, as far as it goes. But brother, listen, your ministry could be much wider. Maybe AE can be a vehicle for you to go across the world.'

Was he offering me a job? I gulped – I felt I was rapidly getting out of my depth. I decided to remind him of the bad news now, before this went any further: 'Mr Cassidy –'

'Call me Michael,' he interrupted me.

'Michael, I had four months' schooling in my entire childhood. The missionaries at the Dorothea Mission had to work very hard to teach me to read and write. That is how I have got as far as this now. But I do not feel educated enough to dream of going beyond this part of Africa.' This was true. I trembled at the very idea, and for once, thank goodness, Patrick wasn't here to push me out of my depth.

So Michael Cassidy began on me. 'But God can use your testimony on an international basis! AE can equip and build you up!'

I felt confused and certainly scared. 'Give me time pray about this,' I hedged. 'I'll have to ask my wife.'

Michael Cassidy gave me his card. 'Write to me when you've had a think and reached a decision.' Next day he was gone, leaving my head spinning with glimpses of new horizons, and feeling very restless. Even so, it took me several days to drum up courage to mention the matter to Rachel. What was I thinking of, even contemplating a vast change? But the restlessness grew, until finally I put the matter before my long-suffering wife.

'I know things are going well here, and I'm delighted. But I'm nearly forty, and I feel restless. The work is the same vision – evangelising for the church. But there would be such resources, such back-up!' As I said it, I knew I was longing for a change, for a fresh vision, the stimulation of new colleagues, and for the close-knit kind of companionship I had known with Patrick Johnstone. What would he think of this?

'And we'd have a salary and a little house.' I felt giddy at the mere thought of a little home of our own.

I suppose I half expected Rachel to rise to the bait of a home of her own, and to be excited and flattered by Michael Cassidy's magnificent offer. Instead, 'You want to leave the Dorothea Mission? After all they've done for you? Your own mother has now gone through Soteria and is a children's evangelist! How could you?' She was incredulous. 'I am prepared to die in the Dorothea Mission,' my wife said with quiet dignity. And that was that.

Crushed, I crept off to fill God in on the latest developments. 'Lord, Rachel says no. So what do I do? Nothing. I can't do this without her agreement. You'll have to speak to her if you want us to move.' There the matter rested, except that I also wrote to Patrick.

To my surprise and relief, he was very positive and encouraging, advising me to 'go for it', as long as I was not leaving the Dorothea Mission for a negative reason. But Rachel would not leave at all.

Weeks flew by, and then several months. We were busy with missions, and I was away a lot. On my return one evening Rachel met me at the doorway. 'Stephen, we must move.'

'What?' Had her mother thrown us out?

'We must join African Enterprise.'

I stood there, dazed and fatigued and astonished, and wondered not for the first time why women have this tendency to plunge into serious conversation the moment their husband walks up the front path.

However, this was indeed important, so I tried to rise to the challenge. 'Why? What has happened to change your mind?' I sank my weary, sandy limbs into a chair outside and gulped gratefully at the cold drink the children brought me.

'Nothing has happened. I just know now that we must go.' All my efforts to get her to talk it out logically failed. Rachel was simply as for it as she had once been against it. Women!

Then another thing happened. I'd gone to some church services in Blantyre where the sermon was not only interminable, but very disappointing. The preacher was saying that God and eternity are a complete mystery to us, and that to be sure of your salvation is an arrogance. We must continue to talk about God and gradually grope to a salvation – maybe.

I found it hard to take. If when I'd been a gang member, Shadrach had told me to grope for God, but not to expect to find anything, I'd have lobbed a petrol bomb and not thought twice about it. It was only the amazing fact of Jesus' life, death and resurrection, and the certainty of his love and forgiveness and an eternity where all would come right that had any power at all in the market-places where I first preached.

To quiet my growing frustration, I reached for my Bible. It fell open on my knees at Isaiah 55 and I read: 'I will send you to the nations that you do not know.'

I nearly dropped the book – the words leapt off the page at me with such force. I had always been taught to live my faith by quiet, daily readings of the Bible, not to pick and choose verses, as you'd choose sweets in a shop. But this was different. I had a feeling of absolute assurance that this one was meant for me now.

'Lord,' I prayed, 'what are these nations that I do not know?' And of course African Enterprise kept coming to mind. My mind was buzzing and I didn't hear another word of the sermon, but the poor man must have groped his way to some sort of finish, because at some point we all went home – me to a sleepless, excited night.

Rachel and I lay and whispered about it for hours among our sleeping children. Her gentle face beamed with joy in the soft candlelight.

Next day we sent off a neat letter written in my vintage Patrick Johnstone style to Michael Cassidy. A letter came right back with an invitation to go to Nairobi in January 1982 and meet the International Partnership Board, who were interviewing for a new evangelist. An airline ticket accompanied it: Michael Cassidy meant business.

When I got there I had a nasty shock: there was another candidate – a highly educated Ghanaian. I know he was highly educated because he told me his story while we were waiting to be called. I skated over my own past, and a sense of doom settled over me. This man was of high calibre. The old panic of being out of my depth swept over me. Why had they bothered to fly me up and then humiliate me? All my optimism was eclipsed and I felt clammy and sick with the emotional pain and embarrassment of inadequacy. I sat and bounced a table-tennis ball gently against a wooden bench and moped. I wanted to go home there and then.

Stephen Mung'oma, an evangelist from Nairobi, found me hunched in the corner. After he'd made sure that I wasn't sickening for something, he did his best to soothe me. 'Brother, God got you here – why not leave it to him and the AE Board?'

The Board spent ages with the Ghanaian, and all the time I brooded and wondered if I was going to be sick.

Then it was my turn. Never have I felt less inspired. I was hoarse and trembling. The International Partnership Board of African Enterprise! I had to convince them I was good enough, when I felt so inadequate. It was hopeless – a warm gesture on Michael Cassidy's part, nothing more.

After gentle enquiries they steered me on to the subject of my testimony. Well, on that at least I was on sure ground, and told it simply, from my heart. They rounded off with a few minutes of questions on my current ministry.

Then it was back to the table-tennis ball, until Bertha Graham, a member of the South African team, came to give us the letters of decision from the Board. The **Ghanaian opened his and sighed. 'Maybe a future date.'**

That did it. 'Then I'm not even opening mine,' I told myself. 'And I want to get out of here.' I rushed to the airport and caught the next flight back to Malawi.

I could not wait to get home. I owed Rachel an apology. She had been right at the first, my dear wife. Our future lay with the Dorothea Mission and I was crazy ever to think differently.

'Well?' Rachel met me at the door. Sadly I kissed her.

'No.'

'No?'

'The Board makes the decisions, not Michael Cassidy alone, and they are tough. They turned away even an educated man.'

Rachel's glance warned: 'Don't start that now.' But she merely said, 'But they invited you. How did they say no? What did they tell you was wrong?'

I tossed the unopened letter on the table. 'It's all in there.'

'But you haven't opened it!'

'No,' I said. She glanced at me. 'You know what I'm like about failing things. I'm off to town now for some errands.'

On return a few hours later Rachel was again waiting impatiently for me, tapping the open letter in her hand. She flew to the car. 'You have been accepted, you dear crazy man!'

'What!'

'It is in the letter.' She shoved it into my trembling hands. I sat there and read the heart-warming, gracious words over and over: 'The International Board of African Enterprise has great pleasure in offering you a place on the AE team. You will spend two years on an orientation team in Harare, before returning to Malawi to join an AE presence in that country.' Sheer waves of delight and joy swept over me. I could not believe it.

'I will send you to the nations that you do not know.'

God's promise to me was coming true.

All the same, it was a wrench to have to say goodbye to the Dorothea Mission. I gave them a nine-month notice in order that they might have time to prepare a new leader for their Malawi team. They were horrified when they heard I was leaving, and even flew Hannes Joubert up from South Africa to try and talk me out of it. I greeted my old friend and colleague warmly, but told him as gently as I could that my mind was made up. When he saw that this was so, we prayed together, and he wished me well.

CHAPTER SEVENTEEN

AFRICAN ENTERPRISE

In May 1982, after nineteen very happy years with the Dorothea Mission, I joined African Enterprise. A new era in my life was about to begin: I was excited at the prospect of wider horizons. Patrick and Jill, after the initial shock at my news, were full of joy for us. I went on ahead to Harare to prepare the way for the family. Rachel and the children packed up our little home, and said sad farewells to friends and family.

On my arrival at the bright and spacious offices of African Enterprise in Harare, I was summoned into the team leader, Chris Sewell's office for a 'settling in' chat.

He asked me first how my search for a house was going. I told him that I had spent two days looking, and which townships I had visited. I sighed. 'It is quite difficult to find something suitable as I have to look out for Rachel and the children as well.'

Chris Sewell looked at me in astonishment. 'Stephen, whatever are you doing going house-hunting in the townships?'

'Well, where else would I go?' I was black, and had always lived in the township of Highfield.

'Well, you look in the suburbs, of course,' said Chris. He saw my amazement, and continued. 'Stephen, we do not segregate here. You will live in an AE-owned house in one of the white neighbourhoods.'

I was thunderstruck. This was unheard of – surely blacks lived in black neighbourhoods?

'Not any longer. The main thing is that you are now an AE evangelist, and need an AE home.' And so Chris gave his administrator the immediate job of looking through the estate agents' adverts and finding me a suitable home.

When they showed it to me I just could not believe my eyes: a cheerful bungalow and huge garden in the former all-white suburb of Eastlea. To white eyes it would have been simply a nice clean bungalow in a pleasant garden. To me it offered space and air and light undreamed of. I was used to living in one room with a wife and five children.

I wandered around my new home. It seemed like a vast palace. I chuckled softly to myself in glee. Then, with a pang, I recalled thirty years before when a little boy had wandered these neighbourhoods in ragged shirt and shorts and peered into dustbins and stared in awe at the black servants. Had I ever eaten at this house's dustbin? Had I ever peeped over the fence and envied the servants of this house for their clean clothes and food? As a gang member I had dreamed of having one like this when the nationalists took over. Now it was my house!

I thought of that verse: 'Seek ye first the kingdom of God, and all these things will be added unto you,' and felt tears scald my eyes. My heart was full to bursting with thanks to God for these easier times, made possible by the incredible generosity of Christians around the world who were willing to support mission in Africa.

Ever a dramatist, I wanted to surprise my family. So when they arrived a month later I said, 'Yes, we have a house. It is one room, like back home in Malawi. I'll take you there now but on the way we will visit a new white friend of mine.' I drove them to the house.

'Oh Stephen, he must be very grand,' said Rachel in a small tired voice, as she looked at the house. 'But no one is here.'

'Let's go in anyway.'

'Oh Stephen, is that wise?' Rachel was timid and dubious, but the kids were so curious that she at last gave in. I unlocked the front door and let all six of them stream past me.

'Ooh! What a beautiful place!' The kids were pop-eyed with wonder. Rachel looked about in awe at the comfortable sofa and table and chairs and curtains. 'We must be very careful not to touch anything,' she called to the children.

I could keep it up no longer. Grabbing my wife in a great bear-hug I shouted, 'This is ours! Welcome to your new home!'

General clamour and wonder broke out in the Lungu family. Rachel tiptoed round the house with tears streaming down her cheeks while the kids screamed their delight at the prospect of sleeping in beds of their own instead of rolled in a series of blankets underneath ours.

My family taken care of, I began my work as an evangelist with African Enterprise. After a warm welcome by the Harare team leader, Chris Sewell, I was given a desk in the evangelism office. I was to be one of a team of three full-time evangelists. My morale soared. How wonderful to have colleagues and office back-up staff. With such organised support, surely anything could be accomplished!

The head of my evangelism team, Chris Sewell, and I soon discovered that we had met before: under very different circumstances, before either of us were Christians. We discovered this by accident while driving to Mutare with another AE leader, a Canadian, Dave Richardson, for a crusade. It was a long drive, and Dave suggested that in order to get to know each other better, we share our testimonies with each other. Chris and I began, and were reminiscing about narrow escapes we had had in our lives when I casually mentioned a time when I and some other Youth League members had done our best to stone the former prime minister of Rhodesia, Sir Edgar Whitehead, during a political rally at the Cyril Jennings Hall, and nearly got shot in the process.

Chris rounded on me in amazement. 'What! Were you there that day?'

'Yes. Do you mean you were too?'

'I was one of the security staff!' (I learned later that Chris had in fact been a chief detective inspector in the Rhodesian Police.) 'I might have shot tear gas at you – if that was you?'

'Yes, it was. I mean, it could have been. The security people did shoot at us with tear gas. You almost got me. Or somebody did.' I could still remember the stench of the tear gas, and the way it had made me cough. We looked at each other and marvelled at how life had changed for both of us.

When you discover that your immediate boss once did his best to tear gas you, you feel right away that you have something in common. Whether it was that, or merely the charming way Chris had with him, I fitted right into the team. I took to evangelism AE-style like a gazelle to the green veldt in spring. The horizons were indeed broader, and the organisational support available meant I could spend time on preparing to preach instead of chasing rumours of chairs and tents and PA systems around the town before meetings.

There were missions going on all the time, and soon I

was working alongside evangelists throughout Zimbabwe, Mozambique, Swaziland, Malawi and Zambia. It was a delight to work alongside other Christians who had also been converted from unpromising backgrounds and then called by God to this marvellous and holy work. We liaised constantly with churches, and preached in schools, factories, market-places and other public places in order to try and reach people with the gospel who otherwise would not hear it. Our knowledge of what our own lives would have been like without Christ gave us an extra urgency to save others from such an unhappy fate.

One highlight of this time for me were various opportunities to preach in the gold-mines of Zimbabwe and South Africa. My father had worked in a gold-mine, and so I had always been curious about them.

Our AE team soon worked out a simple plan. We would approach the manager of the gold-mine and politely ask, 'Mind if we preach?'

Almost always they were astonished, and then intrigued, and then determined to be as polite in return. 'Go ahead. Which of the men do you want to speak to?'

'All of them.' Eyebrows would go up, but the response was if we wanted to wear ourselves out, that was our problem. Often we would be allowed to go down in the cage into the mine itself, and speak to the men during their tea break.

We'd begin with a friendly chat, showing interest in the work and asking them to show us around. We'd remark how deep it was – not a nice place to build a house! This would raise a chuckle from the men, and having got their interest, we'd add that we were Christians, and that we had found that when a person is separated from God, it is like living away deep down in the cold, dark isolation of a mine. Far from warmth and love and sunshine, and totally unnatural. We'd say that God never meant anyone to live permanently in the cold and dark, and that he wanted to give a heavenly mansion to anyone who wanted it. We'd end by offering to pray with anyone who wanted their heavenly Father's house. We'd tell them where our tent meetings were – near their football ground or whatever.

After their shift, many would come over out of curiosity. Many stayed for the meetings. Many awoke to the love of God for even them, miners, and booked that heavenly home for themselves.

The only hitch with these gold-mines was that work went on twenty-four hours a day, and it was easy to get carried away with enthusiasm. Sometimes, after a long day followed by an evening meeting at the tent, I would find it irresistible to drift back over to the mines and pop down to have a chat with the men on the midnight shift. Suddenly, about 1 am, my fatigue would catch up with me, and I'd still be many hundreds of feet below ground in a mine-shaft.

Back above ground, we sought other ways of contacting people who might otherwise never hear about Christianity. We hit on the idea of visiting football games and chatting to people on the sidelines during quiet moments in the game. In this way I fell into the unusual situation of buying tickets for games I did not watch, in order to offer Christian literature to people who were also not watching, and talk with anyone who showed interest.

Everything went fine for some months, until August 1982 when I was part of a crusade to Mutare in Zimbabwe. It was a large mission, and even AE leaders from the USA came along as observers. Apparently one of the things they observed was me, and suddenly I learned that they wanted me to come on a preaching tour of the United States.

I was horrified. I told Michael Cassidy, 'I've seen these Americans in action in Zimbabwe. They are too high for me. I could never do it.'

Michael smiled and said to leave things to him. I hoped he would be too busy to do anything more.

Then one morning in October 1982, I arrived at my desk to find a telex from Michael Cassidy. 'Am on a mission in the Sudan. Come and join me.' Chris Sewell grinned at me and said, 'You'd better get going!'

I was aghast. 'You are the leader in the evangelism department – shouldn't you have gone instead?'

Chris only gave me his warm, relaxed smile. 'Michael wants you. Apart from you translating for him in the Mutare mission, he hasn't had much of a chance to work with you yet. Now off you go!'

Back home Rachel was excited and would not let me get too frightened as I began to pack and do the rounds of the various government departments. Visas, passports, tickets – the paperwork never ended. I watched all those stamps go in with mounting trepidation. This was it: my first-ever preaching trip out of the little cluster of countries I knew so well. And to work more closely alongside Michael Cassidy! He was a renowned evangelist with an international reputation. Suppose I let him down? Suppose he became secretly disappointed in me?

From the moment I met up with Michael in the Sudan, my fears evaporated. Working with him was sheer joy. I loved it and only wished it need never end.

Michael Cassidy is that unusual combination of a man who is quite outstanding at his work, yet somehow never makes you feel inferior. From the moment we stepped onto that platform together, I felt his encouragement as a tangible force. He would push me forward and build me up constantly. Just being with him taught me so much. You could not help but love the man, he only wanted the best for you. He was always the first to say, 'That was great, Steve!'

So when, at the end of the Sudan mission, he took me

aside one evening and said he thought I'd do fine in America, and that it really was important that I should go and talk about the work in Africa and my part in it, I found myself to my astonishment agreeing to the proposed trip. Michael's belief in me had given me more confidence than I would have thought possible.

The trip to the States was to be early 1983. As the plane touched down at last in New York, I clung on to Michael's last words to me: 'Don't worry Steve, just be yourself.' I only hoped that would be enough to satisfy people.

My private worries were at this point interrupted by a most baffling thing. The captain referred to the time in New York as we taxied to a halt, and to my profound astonishment, it was only two hours later than it had been when we left Europe. But we had been on the plane for hours! No one had thought to tell me about international time zones and I emerged from that plane thinking the whole thing smacked of witchcraft.

An AE representative met me at JFK airport. Before I had time to ask him about the mysterious time-keeping of the Americans, another extraordinary thing happened: outside the airport it was white everywhere. Everywhere. And more was falling from the sky. You probably have to be born and grow up in Africa to have the wonder of the thing really hit you.

I gasped. 'What is that?'

'Snow.' My companion grinned. 'Surely you've heard of it?'

I had heard of it, but had not been able to imagine anything like this New York snowstorm. 'Can I touch it?' I whispered.

'Of course,' my companion smiled.

So I dabbed at it and then drew back in a hurry. 'It's cold!'

And that was the beginning of several culture shocks.

Everything was on a scale and luxury and speed beyond my imagining, from the Assembly Hall at the United Nations to the remote control on my host's garage door, not to mention the size of his house.

The Americans gave me a warm and enthusiastic welcome, and within hours of my landing in New York had me launched into my first speaking engagement. I was torn between gratitude that so many American Christians should venture out into a snowstorm to hear a fellow from Malawi talk about his faith, and a growing desire simply to go to sleep. This mystified me, as I still had not got to the bottom of the international time zones business. Many people are affected by jet lag when flying, and I was one of them. I looked out over my first American audience, realised how highly sophisticated they were, and how much they hoped for from me, and prayed that this dazed feeling would soon wear off.

It did. At 2 am that morning I was suddenly wide awake. I lay in bed and read my Bible and prayed to know the reason for my strange wakefulness.

Next morning I discovered the reason why America leads the world in most things. The energy and dedication they give to work has to be seen to be believed. I had expected to speak every day, but was startled to find my speaking itinerary following the clock with almost military precision: 10 am, 2 pm, 3 pm, 5 pm, 7 pm. Students, young wives, young mothers, old wives, grandmothers, young men, retired men, children, every conceivable grouping and some inconceivable. Within a few days I'd met them all. And so it went for six weeks, right across the States. Soon I had the odd sensation of standing still while all these scenes and churches and congregations whirled by me at ever-increasing speed. The Americans themselves were wonderful: their friendliness to me was astonishing.

Everywhere I went I met good-looking people, shining with health, overwhelming hospitality, attentive faces, welcoming churches, luxurious food and beds that seemed a crime to waste time sleeping in.

But such a huge nation! From New York to Vancouver we went, via just about everywhere. Chicago, Denver, Minneapolis, Los Angeles all came and went – everywhere that had churches who supported African Enterprise, and who were able to offer a welcome to an evangelist from AE. They might have wanted to meet a Malawian evangelist, but I could not wait to see the headquarters of the evangelist, Billy Graham, which was in Minneapolis. He had long been a hero of mine.

Planes, cars, taxis and more planes. I discovered I was not the intrepid traveller I had thought, and felt overwhelmed and exhausted at times. Once I fell asleep on a plane and woke up and for a moment could not remember what I had left or where I was flying to or even why. It was a most peculiar feeling – just being Stephen, flying along under a night sky full of strange, northern stars.

But for all my foreign experiences, I was encouraged to find that the Americans seemed to respond to what I had to say. I had worried greatly that my testimony was just too raw and uncouth for such wealthy and educated people. But when I thought of what I could do about it, I decided I could do nothing: my love for Jesus and my story of how he had found me was all I had to give, so I would give that and pray that they would be able to find him too. I was greatly encouraged to find that God did use what I had to offer, as in state after state across that huge country, people wept and decided to seek him for themselves. As I preached one evening in New York, a young man jumped up and came forward. Then another and another. I didn't even get a chance to finish my testimony.

Time and again I was amazed at how people responded and wept. Why should they care about my story? I knew it was not me that they were weeping at, but rather the evidence of God's love and grace at work in my life.

An AE colleague from Uganda, Bishop Festo Kivengere, met up with me in New York where he was preaching. I confessed I was shy at preaching to the Americans. Bishop Festo gave me some valuable guidance: 'Steve, simply share your testimony. Don't worry about high theology. Your ministry is evangelism, and your most powerful tool is your testimony. You are a gifted evangelist, and you have a powerful message.' Then we prayed together and I felt encouraged.

I was happy to share my testimony, but there were times when it was surprisingly difficult to do so. I was experiencing the great American church service programme and discovering that the guest preacher is often wheeled on near the conclusion of the evening, and expected to give more of an epilogue than a talk. After flying all those thousands of miles from Malawi, and then another two thousand or so miles across the States, I found it frustrating to sit through music and announcements for forty minutes and then be asked to speak for five to ten minutes.

One night I rebelled. How could I speak of my Jesus who had saved me, in five minutes? I rebelled as politely as I could. When introduced, I stood up and said, 'You Americans have been blessed with wristwatches but you don't have much time. We Africans have no wristwatches, but we have plenty of time!'

They laughed and I took that to mean that they wouldn't mind if I took longer than ten minutes to tell my story. So I took a deep breath and preached for an unprecedented forty minutes. Back home forty minutes would have been warming up, but here it was unheard of. That night several people came forward for prayer, and one dear lady hugged me and said, 'You could have gone on for ever. It was wonderful!'

Soon my whirlwind American tour came to an end. Four months later I boarded a plane for Amsterdam, where Billy Graham was convening a worldwide congress for Third World evangelists like me. Amsterdam '83 was a heaven-sent opportunity for us to pause and re-examine our calling before God. We learned new approaches in evangelism from each other, and gained tremendous encouragement in seeing that we were part of a vast worldwide family of evangelists, carrying on the work of Christ in every corner of the globe. Isolation was a big problem for many of us – I had been lucky to find the Dorothea Mission and then African Enterprise.

Amsterdam '83 was a watershed in my ministry. It confirmed for me that the gospel is for all peoples, rich or poor. No one is above its demands, and no one is below its loving grace. I had always felt confident in challenging my fellow Africans, but had felt a bit daunted in speaking of sin and repentance to vast meetings of well-heeled Americans. Now I knew that I was the messenger, that the message was from God, and it was the same for everyone. Black or white, rich or poor we were all sinners and all loved by God.

This lesson would be reinforced when I preached with other experienced AE evangelists such as John Wilson and Bishop Festo Kivengere. Always gracious, but never softening their essential message in order to please an audience.

Then it was back to Africa, where in August 1983 I joined up with a large AE team led by Michael Cassidy and his South African team to help out at the great crusade in Blantyre. My goodness, what a crusade! I was still on a high from my trip, and for the duration of the entire mission I don't think I touched ground once. Thousands upon thousands of people turned out to hear our evening meetings, at which Michael Cassidy preached. During each day I preached to dozens of people in schools, factories, market-places and – a new one for me – supermarkets. The manager of one agreed to let me have a few minutes with the staff every morning for a week before they opened their doors for business. Maybe he thought it would increase honesty and decrease any petty crime. Several of the staff then came along to our evening meetings.

As the weeks went by, several thousand people in Blantyre were converted, and we hit the national newspapers. 'Now Blantyre is a born-again city' the headlines announced. This was a bit of journalistic hype, but all the same, everyone was astonished and moved by the tremendous spiritual openness of the people, and by the degree of freedom His Excellency The Life President, Kwadzi, Dr H. Kamuzu Banda's government gave to us. (A long title for the president, but one which was used daily in our press and on the radio. Malawi had no television at this time.)

On the closing afternoon of the great Blantyre mission, Michael invited me not only to share the platform with him, but to share the sermon! He suggested we speak on Isaiah 1:18: '"Come now, let us reason together," says the Lord. "Though your sins are like scarlet, they shall be as white as snow; though they are red as crimson, they shall be like wool."' We agreed that I would preach the first half of the sermon, and that he would preach the second half. And so we did, and it was marvellous – a very happy memory in my life.

So that was 1983. Then in 1984 I was invited to go to Australia for six weeks. Another whirlwind tour of another vast continent. So many memories of new Christian friends, churches, meetings and highways as we toured that huge country.

That year, 1984, also saw the first West African AE mission to Monrovia, Liberia. I helped Dave Richardson to set it up, and in the process we became close friends. Then I preached at many of the meetings in the campaign. Liberia is the home of the descendants of the freed slaves from the cotton fields of the USA, and has quite a different feel to it than other African countries.

In 1985 I was off again, back to the States and also Canada. This time I was prepared for the time difference! And again, I enjoyed my time with the American Christians.

Back in Harare in late 1985, I found there were new plans afoot. Michael Cassidy and other members of the International AE Partnership Board had decided that the time had come to establish a small but permanent AE team in Malawi. With the people so receptive to Christianity, the work would be well worth while. Malawi church leaders had made it clear that they would welcome such steady support.

Michael Cassidy looked around for an appropriate person to take this on. He decided on me, and the Board agreed. I was overwhelmed with the honour of the confidence they were putting in me, and wildly excited at the challenge. I loved Malawi, and I loved AE and to serve as an AE team leader in Malawi was the highest privilege I could imagine. My life seemed to be coming full circle: last time I'd moved from Salisbury to Blantyre to set up an outpost for the Dorothea Mission. Now we were going to live in the Malawian capital city of Lilongwe and set up an outpost for African Enterprise, and I had the benefit of years more experience, plus financial, administrative and prayer support.

Rachel was delighted at the news: we were going home again.

CHAPTER EIGHTEEN

INTERNATIONAL TRAVELS

Not many people would have been enthusiastic about a move to Malawi in 1985. Life was very hard there. President Hastings Banda's government was repressive, and disliked people whose work involved much travel and public meetings: we were often suspected of organising a political uprising. The economy was in very poor shape, and buying everyday necessities was a great challenge at times. Poverty was widespread.

Still, life for the Lungu family had improved out of all recognition. Never again would we have to live seven to a room in Rachel's mother's house; we had a little bungalow in Lilongwe all to ourselves. I had a regular salary, plus two colleagues, Jeremiah Chienda and Songe Chibambo, and a budget from which to organise our crusades.

Our aim, as everywhere in African Enterprise, was to serve as a handmaid to the churches. We could offer them our specialist expertise in evangelism, train elders in how to disciple others, and build a ministry of reconciliation among chiefs, political leaders and church leaders. There was no limit to the need for such a work, and we found the people welcoming and receptive.

Soon our year fell into a regular rhythm based around the weather. From May to September it was the dry season and open-air missions abounded. But come October and the rains, we went inside and concentrated on small group evangelising, and church-based teaching. It was hard to say which approach was the more effective; every 'success' story warmed our hearts and encouraged us to carry on.

Like the time we were holding an open-air outreach in Mutare, Zimbabwe. We had set up our loud speakers on two large rocks near a railway line, and I was preaching to a large crowd. As I spoke, I could see in the distance a young woman going by, holding her baby in a peculiar manner across her hip – head dangling out in front, and legs wriggling behind. She seemed oblivious to her child's discomfort as she walked along. She slowly disappeared over the hill, we had our service, and closed. We were packing up the equipment and my colleagues were coun-selling people, when I suddenly noticed that the young woman and her baby were back again. She approached me and asked: 'Why do you want to know where I am going to spend eternity?'

I stared at her in astonishment. I stammered: 'I was preaching about Jesus because we are Christians.'

Slowly her story came out. She was married to a harsh husband who brought home prostitutes. In despair that afternoon, she had come out to throw herself in front of a train. She had passed our meeting, and was standing by the humming rails, waiting for the next train, when my voice over the PA system had demanded of her: 'Where will you spend eternity?'

The train swung around the corner, and the steel wheels thundered towards her, but she did not jump.

My question thundered in her head. At last she had decided to come back and ask me what I was talking about.

We led her to Christ that morning, and were careful to maintain follow-up care of her at a local Christian's house. She then asked for help in dealing with her husband.

'Stay with him and love him. Feed this prostitute when she comes,' we said.

'This is hard, what you are asking of me!'

'Do it – and you may bring your husband to Christ.'

So the young mother did it. Her husband was mystified by her behaviour, and it unsettled him. She would cook him wonderful breakfasts, and then humbly ask permission to go to church. He would give it, but then follow her. Her behaviour was so inexplicable to him, that he suspected she might have taken on a boyfriend herself. But when he followed her – it was straight into church.

I was a guest preacher at the church again that morning, and preached on marriage. I said that men who abuse and beat their wives are little more than beasts. The husband went home in a huff. When his wife returned from church he hit her so hard that he knocked out a tooth. 'You told the preacher about me!' he raged.

The following week the wife went to church, and again her husband followed her. A different preacher stood up and began talking about marriage and love.

In a little while the husband disrupted the service by running forward and stopping the preacher. 'My wife is here. Where is she?' he shouted.

The young wife gave her baby to a friend to hold. 'Now I am going to be beaten in church,' she said. She walked to the front.

But her husband embraced her instead and burst into tears. 'Forgive me. Forgive me!' He became a Christian.

About this time, I received another invitation to go to Australia on a preaching tour of many of the AE-supporting churches. It seemed that AE had been very pleased with the reception of my American tour, and believed that I could communicate the vital work in which African Enterprise was engaged in Malawi.

From the start, the tour was a success – at least as far as I was concerned. I was prepared for the sort of schedule I would face, and learned how to pace myself. The Australians themselves reminded me of the Americans, warm, and welcoming and rich. Except that the accent was different! Like the time an Australian greeted me with the phrase, 'Have you come here to die?' It took me aback – until I realised that she meant '*today*'.

I preached in large cities and small towns, in churches, in schools, in the open air. It was a delight to share with these friendly people what was happening to the church in Malawi. They taught me some strange Aussie songs with words like billabong, and I retaliated by teaching them Malawian choruses.

I certainly met a cross-section of people: I had tea with the Archbishop, Sir Marcus Loane and his wife in Sydney, and led a drug addict to Christ on the back streets of Perth.

Back in Malawi, I had as many local missions as the team and I could handle. We three evangelists were constantly out on the road, evangelising in schools, factories, colleges, mines, parks and the market-places. In towns we'd attract up to several thousand people. Other missions were bigger, and held in the cities. These could attract up to 15,000 people.

One such mission in Tanzania was the great Dar es Salaam Back-to-God Crusade for which several AE teams collaborated. Our rallies were held in a huge open park on the outskirts of the city. The people in the distant high-rise flats had a bird's-eye view of the proceedings, and hung out of their windows to hear our sermons. When I stood to address the vast crowd on that last day, my heart swelled within me; I wanted nothing but to preach for all my life.

Not that preaching was easy; it wasn't. Whatever the size or shape of the mission, I had long ago discovered a certain pattern of preparation in me. If I was the main preacher, the night of the first meeting I was always nervous. The responsibility of the work before me laid heavily on me. Beforehand I would always kneel and cry to God for wisdom and the right words. Once the service was under way, I would be eager to speak. The only difficulty then was that sometimes the programme was too crowded, and I would not even stand to speak until well over an hour (or even two) into the meeting. That is a long time to sit on a platform looking enthusiastic and relaxed but gradually becoming tired, and knowing that ever before you was the enormous job of having to hang on to a flagging audience late in the evening.

Of great encouragement were the individual stories which kept trickling through to us. Like the man whose wife was dragged along to one my meetings. 'You must go forward!'

'Never my dear. It is not in me.'

After I preached, I gave an invitation as usual. 'Come now, don't let the glue of the devil stick you in your chair. In the name of Jesus, come!' The husband beat everyone else to the front. His wife was a close second, weeping tears of joy.

When you preach and people come forward like that because of something you say, it is very humbling. 'Why should God use me?' I often ask myself. I know my many faults all too well.

On the other hand, when you preach and *no one* comes forward, it is even more humbling! This happens too. Being an evangelist is about being a messenger, not a magician. You don't pull souls out of seats like rabbits out of a hat. There are numerous times when no one responds. I have prayed and preached in tears, giving the message I felt God would have me give – but only getting a stony silence.

One time this happened in a town in Bulawayo, and I was so devastated that I went home and burst into tears. Some months later I was back in town, with the memory of that difficult evening still an unpleasant shadow. I had just packed up my AE van, and set off, trying to drive and drink a bottle of coke at the same time. Then I heard shouts, and a man weaved towards me on a bicycle. 'Hey, Stephen Lungu! Stephen Lungu!' I stopped and pulled over. His face wore a broad grin. 'Do you remember me?'

I shook my head. 'I am sorry,' I began, 'but . . .'

'Never mind. I was at the crusade on the last day, when you preached about the second coming, and no one responded.'

I winced. 'Yes, that was a difficult night.'

'It certainly was. I was drunk. When I got home I couldn't sleep a wink because of what you'd said. By the next morning I'd given in and gave my heart to the Lord.'

I hugged him for joy and laughed. 'My missing convert!'

'Well I tried to tell you all the next morning, but by the time I got in from the township and out to your tent, you were all packed and gone!'

This problem of preaching and getting no response was one that I had to work through and pray through. I wanted something from God that would help me keep the thing in perspective. In time, God gave me a passage from Habakkuk which has been of enormous help to me over the years: 'Though the fig-tree does not bud and there are no grapes on the vine, though the olive crop fails and the fields produce no food, though there are no sheep in the pen, and no cattle in the stalls, yet will I rejoice in the Lord,

I will be joyful in God my Saviour' (3:17–18). When I read this passage, I knew that an evangelist is a messenger, and I must leave the results to God. All that is required of me is to be faithful, not successful.

One highlight of the late 1980s for me was a chance to go to the UK and meet up with Patrick Johnstone. While I was there, he took me with him to Scotland, where we ministered together at a Christian conference. It was the fulfilment of a dream we had had together since the 1960s – to minister as brothers not just in my country, but also in his!

By the late 1980s Rachel could spare more time from our five children. While I was often out of town on missions, Rachel had got her eye on an opportunity for evangelism much closer to hand: marriage-guidance counselling. That may sound bizarre, but life in Malawi was very hard, with little education, few jobs and widespread poverty. Under such social pressures, families did not thrive. At a time when men and women and children most needed the loving security a good marriage provides, they were tearing their marriages apart.

Rachel began by making friends with the Christian wives nearby. Several had husbands who were not Christians. She gave them help and support and prayer, and through the wives, several of these husbands became Christians. We invited them to our home for fellowship and we all enjoyed it so much that this soon became a regular thing. Somehow more husbands and wives kept getting involved, and before long several local churches asked us to hold a series of meetings on Christian marriage.

Rachel and I had mixed enough with Western culture by now not to be ashamed to talk of the more intimate side of marriage, which is a taboo subject in Malawi, and about which there is much ignorance. We decided our talks would be based on the Christian view of marriage as laid out in the Bible, and include some basic sex education, the need for constant communication, the proper place of in-laws, the budgeting of money, the extended family and – most important – the place of the wife: slave or partner?

Our talks greatly embarrassed some people, but apparently enlightened them too. Certainly no one was too embarrassed not to come along: soon we had more people than we could get into the churches. So we held some more meetings. Then people asked when they were going to be held again, and we began to realise we had stumbled on a real need here. Soon our marriage-guidance counselling had become a regular fixture of our work during the rainy season. Over the years dozens of men and women have become Christians through the witness of their Christian spouses, and several hundred marriages have been repaired and strengthened.

For me, a great joy in this is when I think of the children who will never have to know what it is to have a violent father, to go hungry so that father can have his beer, to go cold and neglected because mother is too oppressed and downtrodden to care properly for the family. If someone had helped to repair my parents' marriage, how different my early life would have been.

Once on a mission in Karonga, Malawi, I came across three youngsters who had been abandoned, like my brother, sister and I had been. Only in this case the two girls were twelve and fourteen, so they had turned to prostitution to keep themselves and their little brother from starving. Their plight was enough to break my heart. All three became Christians during the mission, and were put in touch with the local church who promised to care for them.

People come to Christ in all sorts of conditions. The drunkest convert I think I've ever had was a Zimbabwean called Patrick. Our AE team was holding an open air meeting in a small town in Zimbabwe late one afternoon, just near a beer hall. As I preached, this young chap came out of the beer hall. His shirt and trousers were askew, and he was walking like sailors walk on a lurching ship, except that he was on dry ground. Slowly, and at all sorts of strange angles, he staggered closer to our little meeting. Then he stopped and stood still, gently swaying. I remember wondering whether he had stopped to listen, or stopped because his legs would not go any further. Anyway, there he stood until I had finished. When I gave the invitation, he raised an arm. This was unwise, as it unbalanced him, and he nearly went over in the direction of his lifted arm. But I went over to him, steadied him and asked, 'Can I help you?'

'I want this Jesus,' he slurred.

'Do you know what you are doing?'

'Yes,' he slurred. 'You see,' he confided, 'I have beer in me, which gives me problems. But you say to have Jesus instead, and all my problems will be over. So – I want him.'

He would not be put off, so I finally invited him to kneel.

'No,' he said.

'Why not?'

'I'll fall over.' This was unquestionably true. So we prayed standing up, and then after a little while he set off again, swaying. An unusual conversion, but it stuck. Next day I visited him at home, and found him sober and wanting to know more. We talked further, and I put him in touch with some mature Christians. Patrick found that Jesus did indeed replace the beer, and today he is the pastor of a thriving Assemblies of God church.

In 1986 Mother received some extraordinary news: my father was still alive and actually living in some village or other near Blantyre. Rachel and I searched, but to no avail, and so we contacted the local chiefs for help. Within a few

days they summoned us to a remote village and led us to a
very old man sitting under a tree and sucking sugar cane. I
stared down at him, and could just about make out my
father. He stared up at me with rheumy old eyes filled with
alarm. He thought I was the police come to arrest him for
something or other.

Gently the chief introduced me. The fear on my father's
face slowly turned to blank wonder, and then memories
came back. He stared and stared at me. 'Stephen. You are
little Stephen. I remember you.'

We both wept, he out of shock, me for the loss of what
might have been. I felt no bitterness – just sorrow and pity
for this poor, sad old man. He had married again a couple
of times more. His current wife was very frail, but at nearly
ninety he seemed likely to stay with her this time. He
wanted to see me and meet Rachel again, and in the following months and years our visits became a regular
thing.

It will come as no surprise to you, my reader, that I
found an opportunity to share my Christian faith with my
father, and had the enormous delight in leading him to
Jesus. It was easier than I might have expected, because
my father's heart had already been touched by the preaching of Shadrach Wame, a local evangelist.

Meanwhile, our AE team's opportunities for evangelism
continued and included some unusual meetings. I was
often reminded of St Paul's strategy of using whatever
chances he could, and becoming all things to all men if in
doing so he might win some to Christ. For example, we
discovered that the way to a professional man's attention
is through his tummy. So we would host a meal at a hotel
to which executives, bankers and government officials
would willingly come (paying towards the cost of the
meal). Then, after they had been mellowed by food, we

would share our faith with them. This worked well during the 1987 Lilongwe-for-Jesus Crusade in Malawi where the senior executives and diplomats of the city turned out for us. It was a fantastic opportunity to share the gospel with these powerful men who rarely had time to think about religion at all.

From fancy lunches I turned to fancy dress, rather to Rachel's disapproval. During the Lusaka Back-to-God Crusade, I decided to use some Egyptian robes and head-dress a friend had given me. The sight of a 'Muslim' preaching Christ stopped a lot of people in their tracks during our visits to the market-place, and several were converted. I was so pleased with this success, that I put my robes back on for my visit to the Zambia Fellowship of Evangelical Students at the University of Lusaka. Here I came unstuck, as the rather conservative students were horrified by my Egyptian attire, and asked me to take them off before I preached. But I had brought no other clothes along, and so we were at a stalemate. In the end, we agreed that I should not speak. It was the one and only evangelistic meeting I've been to where I never said a word. Except that I did close in prayer!

The following year, 1989, I visited Egypt itself for the first time, and worked alongside some Egyptian Christians in Cairo. For this visit I gleefully dug out my Egyptian cos-tume again, in which I thought I looked rather dashing. Rachel stifled a smile at my appearance, but at least the head-gear kept off the sun when I visited the pyramids. Whatever Rachel might say, those robes were a great visual aid to grab attention.

On it went. My team and I liked to think of ourselves as little donkeys carrying Jesus around Africa. Up and down the social ladder we went, eager to preach in any setting that we could. In Swaziland I linked up with Michael

Cassidy to speak at a breakfast meeting for some top executives. Later that morning he was with top government officials, while I had seized an opportunity to preach at a bus-stop terminus before lunch. Dozens stopped to listen and several enquiries were made.

Back in Malawi, I addressed businessmen and government officials myself at a special dinner service in Karonga, and next day was sharing my faith with simple fishermen down with the nets on the shores of the lake. Some time after, in the Salima-for-Jesus Crusade, my team and I took over the local football field and packed it with thousands of adults and children. We would always adapt our approach to the people and the situation, but the message remained the same.

In 1991 my father's final wife died, and as he was now in his nineties, he moved in with us. The burden of caring for him fell rather heavily on Rachel that first year, for 1991 was a travelling year for me. I went to the AE International Conference in Victoria Falls to talk budgets and planning. I am not a great lover of paperwork and welcomed the chances to relax with AE staff on the tennis court. Here I made a valuable new friend: the Reverend Richard Bewes of All Souls', Langham Place in London. I knew this was the beginning of a beautiful relationship when he let me in on a few tennis tips, including what he called the eastern back-hand grip.

Then it was on to Europe, this time for an AE tour of Switzerland led by Michael Cassidy and a couple of other AE evangelists. After missions in Africa, where the whole congregation will sway with the music and let rip with enthusiastic shouts, I found speaking to two hundred Swiss ladies at a Lausanne Ladies' Breakfast an unnerving experience. You could have heard a cuckoo clock tick in the hushed silence that greeted my testimony.

Nothing. I sat down nervously.

Some of the other African evangelists on the tour were also unnerved by Swiss restraint following their years of African expression. The nervous tension boiled over one evening when we Africans went for a walk in the snow and somebody threw a snowball. The four of us went mad and pelted each other with snowballs amid great whoops of laughter. Finally, frozen but completely relaxed, we returned to the hotel as demure a foursome as even a Swiss hotelier could hope for.

Then it was back to Malawi for a busy spring of missions in central Africa, until in 1992 I flew to England for another preaching tour. Jean Wilson, the international treasurer of African Enterprise, and its British co-ordinator, saw that everything went like clockwork, and I had a great time travelling the country and meeting hundreds of AE supporters in various churches. It warmed my heart to see their joy and interest in our work, and I felt somehow that I wasn't making new friends so much as getting acquainted with ones whom I'd not met before.

Back in Malawi, a high point of the year for me was seeing the conversion of some eighty-nine Muslims. When they threw down their little hats to convey their decision to make a total stand for Christ, I felt choked. These were brave, dedicated men, and they would undoubtedly suffer for their decision to convert.

In 1992 came the tragic news that my dear old friend Jill Johnstone had died of cancer in England. I mourned her deeply. Her love and help twenty years ago had kept me true to God's calling when times were rough. I still think of her often as we continue our work. How happy she would be to see all the opportunities we have had to reach out to the common people of Africa whom she loved so much.

Also in 1992 we decided that the AE headquarters in

Malawi would have to move out of my house. It was just too crowded and chaotic. We moved into local offices in Lilongwe for some months, and then were fortunate enough to secure a suite of offices in the Scripture Union building in Lilongwe, where we were happy for many years, and where we could concentrate on outreach.

In one factory the manager agreed to let us speak to his hundreds of staff during their fifteen-minute tea-break. So for three hours a colleague and I addressed fifty people every fifteen minutes. We took it in turns to preach and to counsel. By the time we were finished after three hours of this, we were truly finished! But the excitement of seeing people come to the Lord, just as they were, in their overalls and oil stains, is indescribable.

Then there were our visits to the police stations to preach to the police during their tea-break. No longer am I afraid of them. Instead I pack a very small Bible. I say I am a secret policeman of Christ, pull out the little Bible and declare, 'These are my handcuffs!' They chuckle and listen.

So do thieves. One of our open-air missions attracted a car thief who'd developed a nice line in stealing cars in Zimbabwe, taking them to Malawi to sell, and then stealing them back and running them back to Zimbabwe to sell for a second time. He became a Christian, and the last I heard he is trying to repay the people he has cheated, or at least those he can trace.

Murderers have a harder time making it up to their victims. One man who confessed to eight killings was converted with his switchblade in hand. This appealed to me – I was reminded of me and my petrol bombs years ago, and I spent time after the meeting talking with him. Then, at his request, the team and I went home with him to smash his many calabashes of home-made beer. He said that the beer made him violent and that's why he had killed eight people. His mother watched us sourly – I suspect she liked the beer too.

Another recent convert who is happy to leave her past behind her is a girl converted from witchcraft. In certain ceremonies she had been eating human flesh. Now she is a member of a local church, and building a new life.

At our mission to Ntcheu, Malawi, thousands came to hear us, and 1,500 were converted to Christ. Each conversion is a separate, exciting story of the grace and love of God reaching out to desperate, lonely people who are in great need. Truly, there is no more exciting work on earth than being an evangelist and telling people the good news of Christ.

CHAPTER NINETEEN

A KALEIDOSCOPE OF PEOPLE AND PLACES 1994–2000

I write this final chapter as the year 2000 draws to a close. Looking back on the past few years, I can only thank God for the privilege of sharing the gospel with literally hundreds of thousands of people in many countries and cultures.

My life is nothing if not varied, and here is just a kaleidoscope of memories taken from the past five or six years.

In late 1994 there was African Enterprise's great city-wide mission to Addis Ababa. For weeks we preached in dozens of venues right across the city. Our final two meetings were held out on the racecourse, where there was plenty of room. This was just as well, for by then all Addis Ababa knew about us, and the crowds were enormous. The Government got concerned that such a huge Christian gathering might attract trouble from the Muslim fundamentalists, and sent along a contingent of armed soldiers to keep things calm. Edward Muhima, a colleague from AE, and I shared a platform. He preached on the Saturday, and I preached on the Sunday. We addressed a vast sea of faces. I was told later that we had preached to some 250,000 people.

When I finished preaching, I appealed to anyone who wanted to become a Christian to come forward. In my urgency, I said, perhaps unwisely, '*Run* to Jesus!' Well, they certainly did. To my astonishment, people began to literally run – nearly 10,000 of them. It was an amazing sight. One of the people who rushed forward was a soldier, heavily armed with an AK47 rifle. When he reached the front, a lady counsellor tentatively approached him, asking if she could help. To her alarm, the soldier handed her his heavy rifle, and sank to his knees in prayer. We train our counsellors to be prepared for most situations, but not how to hold AK47 rifles!

Africa is just so open to Jesus. Wherever you go, if you pray and preach, people do respond. The problem is not getting people to listen, but it is sometimes in simply getting to them at all. The vast distances and difficult terrain of Africa demand a variety of methods of travel. Easiest are planes, helicopters, trains, cars, motorbikes, trucks or bicycles. Only when I'm desperate do I resort to donkey or ox-carts in order to reach remote villages. Worst of all are the dug-out canoes, used to cross the swamps of Malawi to reach remote villages. I can't think of a single good thing to say about a dug-out. If you sit very still, you are slowly eaten alive by clouds of mosquitoes. If you try and shake off the mosquitoes, the canoe loses its balance and turns over, dumping you head first into murky, crocodile-infested water.

Flying around America by jet is quicker and far more comfortable. And whereas conversations in dug-outs on vast swamps is usually kept to a few terse comments like: 'Brother, please sit still', or, 'Are you sure this is the right direction?', you can have some deeply personal encounters aboard planes.

Like the time I was flying from Toronto to Chicago, and

was seated next to a very smartly dressed blonde lady. As we took off, I prayed for her silently, as I do for all the strangers I travel with. I prayed for an opportunity to speak to her. It didn't seem likely – she was withdrawn and very frosty. Ice-cream wouldn't have melted in her mouth.

Then suddenly the plane flew into a big storm. Turbulence rocked and rolled that plane. It shuddered and shimmied and did all sorts of wobbly things that planes shouldn't do. Lockers flew open and cases started falling on people's heads. My ice-lady melted fast.

First thing I knew, she had turned to me and latched on tight – her fingers pinching in panic. 'What's this? What's happening?' she panted.

I was so eager to share my faith and comfort her, that I began with a rather tactless: 'Are you ready to meet God?'

She didn't like the implications of this very much. 'Surely it's not as bad as that!' she cried. 'I can't die! We can't die! Tell me no!'

I soothed her as best as I could. When a few minutes later the plane stopped corkscrewing and started flying again, she gradually released her grip on me and we got talking. It turned out that she was already under great emotional strain. She had just left her husband, and now the threat of death in the sky was the last straw. So I shared my story and my faith, and she listened. She must have figured that she had nothing left to lose, and everything to gain, for then and there she became a Christian. We prayed together, and when we eventually landed, she asked me to stay with her until she could phone her husband and make amends. I last saw her booking another plane ticket – to return home.

Poor Americans have great spiritual needs too. In 1996 the scandal about the LA police beating a helpless black man on the highway broke. Soon after, I was in LA with

Chris Sewell, my former team leader from Zimbabwe. Tensions between black and white, police and gangs were running high across the city. The American office of AE looked at Chris and me, and said, 'This is too good to miss.'

So AE USA arranged that we should go into a well-known and respected drug addiction and rehabilitation centre in LA, and share our faith. We were, after all, a white ex-policeman and black ex-gang leader, both from Zimbabwe. We arrived at the centre, and my goodness, even I, who have seen a thing or two in my time, wondered what we had taken on. If those LA drug addicts acted as intimidating as they looked, we were in for a lively evening. But to our astonishment they did listen to our message. Some forty of them even came forward afterwards to talk further with us.

Back in Malawi in May 1997 my father died. He was 104, and he died a committed Christian. He had lived with us for nearly eight years, and he and Rachel were like father and daughter. In old age his past life haunted him, and he kept asking me for the forgiveness I had already given him years before. Rachel and I mourned his going, but gave thanks for a life redeemed by God's love.

In 1998 African Enterprise held its annual Pan-African mission in Ghana. These missions take anything up to two years to put together, and the logistics are staggering. Churches, transport, venues for meetings, follow-up groups, literature, PA systems, prayer groups, etc. The work involved is enormous, but so worth while. Our Ghana Mission March at the end of it was a thrilling climax to weeks of preaching and outreach.

Sometimes preparations can involve you in hilarious moments. Dave Richardson, a Canadian AE member, is a specialist in setting up missions. When he set off for Sierra Leone once to prepare for a mission, he took me along. The

Freetown Christians wanted us to talk to a pastors' conference some distance into the bush. The thirty kilometres took us four hours, and we arrived to find that in our honour a huge steel bed had been prepared for us to share. Neither of us were keen on the idea, but we did not want to offend our hosts.

While we were wondering about this, they offered us some food. We sampled it and nearly choked to death – local cuisine was built around the hottest spices I have ever tasted. At the end of the evening, having finally dined on a chocolate bar Dave found in his pocket, we gingerly climbed onto the great edifice of a bed. We soon discovered the snag – the mattress was so soft that it kept rolling us together in the valley in the middle. For the next two days we survived by nibbling chocolate and hanging on to the respective edges of that bed for dear life. What we do in the name of evangelism!

Since early 1999 I have been carrying a heavy, ornate gold pen around with me. I haven't gone 'flash', nor do I have illusions of grandeur: it was a present from an Egyptian family following a most moving encounter there in February 1999. I was on a mission in Sohag, when a young man came to my room the day after one of my services. He looked terrible. He was bald and thin. He produced a sheaf of papers: they were his doctor's letters saying that he had leukaemia and a few months to live. He was only twenty-four. He wanted me to pray for him. He was crying.

I hesitated. This, I felt, was beyond me. I was an evangelist, not a faith healer. But out of compassion for him, I laid hands on him, and prayed. I didn't even know what to pray – just to present him to God, and ask for Jesus' blessing on him. My hand felt hot as I touched him, but nothing more. He jumped, however, and seemed very alert, muscles tensed, throughout my prayer. He told me later that as I had prayed, he had felt a current like electricity rush through his body.

I shrugged helplessly. I am an evangelist, and God has not given me a ministry of healing. I said goodbye, and wished him well.

A few days later the mission was still going on, and that evening as I was about to preach, the young man marched in. He wouldn't sit down, but kept waving some papers high above his head. He was very excited, eyes sparkling, as he cried: 'Please everybody, may I share something.'

We gave him the floor, and he continued: 'I have been dying of leukaemia. Doctors have told me I had a few months left at most. But a few days ago I was prayed for, and next day I felt so different that I went back to the doctors. They can find no trace of the leukaemia. Nothing. These are the results of my blood tests, and they are clear. I know I have been healed. My doctor says if this isn't a miracle, he doesn't know what is.'

The meeting went crazy that night, and I never did get a chance to preach. Next day the young man's large family arrived at my door, all wanting to thank me and – much better – all wanting to know about Jesus. They gave me the pen, and I keep it as a keepsake of that wonderful answer to prayer. Two years on, the young man is fit and well, and an active Christian.

The high point of 1999 for me was organising the first ever Presidential Prayer Breakfast in Malawi. In the run-up to the elections, Malawi was in a very bad way, with great tensions between the three main political parties. People feared we might be on the brink of civil war.

Some friends and I were very concerned, and spent time in prayer over it. We then felt led to try and organise a Prayer Breakfast – a neutral forum where we could invite all the political leaders to take time out from politics, and come together before God, to pray for the good of Malawi. So we set to work. Our team consisted of: the Rev. Dr Madalitso Mbewe, the Rev. Dr Lazarus Chakwera, the Rev. Mgala, Brigadier Chinjala, Joyce Mlelemba and me.

It was a good thing we had each other, and a strong and stubborn faith, because it took us nearly five months to get the seven political parties together in one room for the first Presidential Prayer Breakfast in Malawi!

Getting the funding was a challenge, until the German embassy generously gave us the money we needed.

Organising the breakfast was a challenge, because the leader of each political party decided it was wisest to bring his own, to prevent us poisoning them(!).

Persuading the President to be there was also a challenge, as he had many reservations about the wisdom of even having breakfast with the opposition. In the end, on the day before the breakfast, he said he would come only if we switched the venue from a large hotel in Lilongwe to the new state house that housed the Parliament. He felt safer that way. 'Choose any large room in there that you like,' he said. So, once we got over the shock, we did.

We had sent a questionnaire to each political leader, asking the same question of each: 'How do you propose to bring peace to Malawi and make the country work together?' We felt it was a fair enough question, and would show them where we were coming from. Malawi's good had to come first, we felt, not the advantage of any one party.

Organising the speaker was a challenge. We had wanted Michael Cassidy or Edward Muhima or one or two others. But everyone was too far away, or already committed. The breakfast was to be on Tuesday morning, and all weekend we prayed for a miracle. By 5 pm on Monday we decided there wasn't going to be a miracle. By 9 pm it became clear

I was going to have to do it.

I went to my room, and suddenly felt very nervous. Now just what had I got myself into? I thought back to the days of Patrick Johnstone and our mission preparation – if only he could see me now! I fervently wished he were here for me to bounce ideas off. But he wasn't, and so I sought God frantically, and prepared until 2 am. Then I went to bed, only to pray until nearly dawn.

The breakfast went splendidly. The leaders and leading representatives of all seven political parties came along. I preached on the power of forgiveness and reconciliation. No one took offence. No one was offended by our questionnaire. And best of all, no one was poisoned! I knew we had succeeded when the President thanked us, and suggested we think of inaugurating a Presidential Prayer Breakfast as an annual event.

In December 1999 it became clear that AE Malawi would have to move offices. Since 1993 we had been happy as tenants in the Scripture Union building in Lilongwe. But they were growing, and so we had to go. It was very sad, because the team ended up in my garage for a while. This was not ideal, but eventually it all worked out for the best. Thanks to the support of Christian friends around the world, we raised a few thousand dollars – enough to build a small three-room office of our own on a piece of land near our homes in Lilongwe.

Millennium Eve was an emotional time for people around the world. It had a bad effect on an accountant in Lilongwe, whose depression was only deepened by the thought of such a momentous occasion. That and the fact that his wife had found out about his numerous affairs and was about to leave him.

The first I knew of it was at 2 am on 1 January 2000 when the phone rang. A man was sobbing. 'Mr Lungu,' he began, 'I am going to kill myself.'

'Er – hello – are you? Why is that? Who are you?' I stammered, waking up fast.

'Life has nothing for me! It's all over for me!' he cried.

'Can we meet?' I suggested.

'Would you come? I've rung two friends, and they told me to wait till morning. But I won't be here in the morning . . .'

'I'll come,' I said. 'Now. Where are you?'

He was a few kilometres away – a few minutes in the car. Or he would have been – except that I suddenly remembered I had no car, having lent it to a friend for the night.

'I'll walk,' I said. 'Expect me there in two hours.'

'I can't wait that long,' he said, 'I'll come to you.'

He was there in fifteen minutes, his wife looking terrified at the speed they had been travelling. The man was so hysterical that he left his wife in the car with the engine still running, rushed into my house – and then just sat there and sobbed, unable to speak. His wife explained that he had a history of suicide in the family – five of his relatives had killed themselves – and that he got very emotional at times.

Rachel and I talked with the couple all night. By the time the sun rose on 1 January 2000, the man and his wife had become Christians. The man was drawing up a list of all the women to whom he would say goodbye. In the days that followed, the couple joined an excellent local church, and within weeks had been called by God to do some prison visiting, which they have been happily doing ever since. A nice twist to the story is that the man went on to lead his father to the Lord – a man that I had witnessed to years before.

As the new century gets under way, African Enterprise continues to grow. AE Malawi is just one of ten AE teams: South Africa, Zimbabwe, Kenya, Uganda, Rwanda, Tanzania, Ghana, Ethiopia, and soon, hopefully, Egypt.

We work as a loose federation of evangelistic teams. We mostly do our own missions, responding to the national and international opportunities that come our way, and that fit our annual budget. But each year the whole of AE joins forces for an annual Pan-African mission, which can be years in preparation and go on for weeks. We also meet up with each other at the International Partnership Boards which are held each year. I value these, and especially the fellowship of the other team leaders. It is a chance to share problems and opportunities, and keep ourselves knit together as a team.

At present, our AE Malawi team numbers four. I'm the team leader, and a fortunate man because I have excellent colleagues. One is Abel Sauti-Phiri, our administrator-evangelist. Abel is a former pastor of Deeper Life Bible Church, and a friend of twenty years' standing. I asked him to join AE just as he was about to ask me the same thing. Abel gave us a bad scare late last year when he fell desperately ill with malaria.

Then there is Martyn Phiri, our technician-evangelist. Martyn is a former radio repair man, and a keen member of his local Assemblies of God church. When I discovered his gift with radios and PA systems, he was a doomed man: I was absolutely determined to get him on our team. We then sent him off for even more technical training at African Enterprise's headquarters in Pietermaritzburg. Martyn is in charge of all our sound and recording equipment at missions, and lives a stressful life. This is because the electrical equipment we can buy in Malawi is almost always faulty and fuses easily. You don't realise how essential electricity is to modern evangelism until you are right in the middle of a large tent meeting, and your congregation is plunged into total darkness or silence. So I made him a happy man at Christmas 2000. I had been in England a few weeks before, with Anne Coomes, finishing off this book, and we made a quick visit to a John Lewis store to buy Martyn some extension cables that actually work.

Morrison Chigamba is our projects manager-evangelist. Morrison was working for the government in various development projects until he retired. He was already one of our board members, and so we brought him in to over-see our small projects. These include training some women in the villages nearby in midwifery, some adult literacy training, and how to bore water-holes.

We sadly lost a staff member to AIDS a few years back. Her story is an illustration of the tragedy facing Africa today. She was a moral, devout Christian woman, but her husband's infidelity meant that he caught AIDS and then gave it to her. She was a frail person, and succumbed quickly. Her husband followed her a few months later.

As with all the AE evangelists, our team belongs to a variety of denominations, and attends a variety of local churches. This commitment is seen as vital, for AE is not a denomination on its own, and each team member is firmly grounded in a local worshipping community. I often get invitations to preach at various local churches, and enjoy doing so. Here I usually preach for two to two-and-a-half hours – Africans would expect nothing less!

I'd like to close this book now in the way I began it – by telling you about my family.

My earliest memories were of my mother, my father, my brother John and my sister Malesi. My mother is now in her mid-seventies, and settled happily in Harare. She has near-ly retired from Christian work, but still enjoys taking the occasional women's meeting. Her life has been transformed by God's love, and she is a happy woman, at peace with herself. Last year she boarded a plane for the first time and flew to stay with us for three months in Lilongwe. We loved having her, and she is very close to Rachel.

My father, as I have said, died in our home at 104 years of age. He was a Christian, and at peace, but still haunted at times by the events of his former life.

My brother John and sister Malesi are sadly not yet Christians. Malesi lives in Zimbabwe, in Tafara township. She is married with four children and works as a home nurse. John never left Lilongwe after Papa took us there as children. He is married with a number of children, and is a truck driver. They had not seen each other for over forty years until Malesi came to visit us and see Papa's grave in Lilongwe. I then introduced them to each other, and said, 'You know each other.' 'Do we?' they asked. 'You are sister and brother,' I replied. They hugged each other and cried.

My mother was always one for surprises, and one of the latest has been to discover that in the years after her separation from John, Malesi and me, she and my father met up again and produced another daughter, Ruth. Then they broke up, but got together for one last time and produced two more daughters, Rhoda and Janet. All three girls were brought up by various relatives of my mother, as we had been.

Aunt M of the chicken coop and her family remained in Highfield. In the years after my conversion, we made up our differences and became good friends. Her family came to mean a great deal to me. I was very sad when Aunt M died six years ago.

Nowadays there are about twelve of us living in the Lungu home at any one time. My eldest daughter Agnes is in London studying computers. James, my eldest son, is in Malawi in marketing. Faith, my second daughter, has gone into childcare. Samuel wants to go to college in the States, and Esther is still at school. Then there are the various grandchildren, as well as a nephew or two, and several other of the seven children we have adopted over the years. People tell me that Rachel and I are the foremost marriage-guidance counsellors in Malawi. Having raised thirteen children in thirty years of marriage we have at least some experience to pass on!

I still travel a good deal. A look through my diary reminds me that in 2000 alone I visited Egypt, South Africa, Nigeria, Australia, New Zealand, Canada, Germany, Holland, Argentina and England, as well as conducting numerous missions in Malawi. And on it goes! We always try to keep a balance between missions in Africa and telling our support churches what is happening in our country and asking for their prayers.

Rachel and I maintain our own inner spiritual lives by constant reading of Christian books and the Bible, and regular prayer and fasting. In addition, I have found a spiritual director, a mature godly man with whom I can share spiritual things. At home, a little group of us fast all day every Friday before a regular all-night prayer meeting that ends early Saturday morning. So we never have to worry about what to do with our weekends!

The church in Malawi is strong and growing, and it is a privilege to head an AE team here. We know that any converts will find good homes in local churches, and be properly cared for. But wherever I preach, from the swamps of Malawi to the streets of Cairo, I find a great thrill of anticipation at what God may do in somebody's life. Truly, there is no more exciting work on earth than being an evangelist and telling people the good news of Jesus Christ.